Healing from Heaven

Volume 1

By Ernest Angley

Healing from Heaven *Volume 1*

All Rights Reserved.
Copyright © 2012 Ernest Angley.
Printed in the United States of America.
Distributed by Winston Press.
P.O. Box 2091, Akron, Ohio 44309
ISBN 978-1-935974-18-5

CONTENTS

INTRODUCTION

I want to begin by saying that this is God's book; and in it, you will find the truth and all you need to know about healing from Heaven. As you read, you will find many scriptures on healing, and God has given me His thoughts and explanations on each one. Through them, God will show many of you step-by-step how to receive miracles you have been longing for; and you will start making those steps even before you realize it. Study them, and they will enable God's light to shine for you through the gifts of knowledge and wisdom the Holy Ghost uses in my life. Then once you have read this whole book, it will be up to you to accept it or reject it.

Now, with heartfelt gratitude and admiration for our Lord, Savior and Healer, Jesus Christ, I give you these great, divine scriptures on healing from Heaven for soul, mind and body. Due to limited space, every scripture concerning salvation for the soul and healing for the body could not possibly be incorporated into this special book; but I believe that if you will carefully and prayerfully study the promises given along with the many other related scriptures that are in the Bible, they will become living reality to you just as they are to me. You will realize that you absolutely can have a miracle. *Thus saith the Lord, many people are going to be healed while reading this book.*

CHAPTER 1

Divine Healing Is Real

I know what divine healing is all about because I went to the edge of the grave when I was just twenty-three years old. I watched my body go down to about a skeleton as more and more of my organs became afflicted; and I got so bad that I thought for sure that I'd be dead in a few more days.

I was suffering so much during a service I was conducting in Florida when a little, old woman jumped out of her seat. She had retired from the ministry and was on fire for the Lord, and He had taken her over. His prophecy for me rolled forth from her lips; and in it, the

Lord said I would be healed. When I accepted that prophecy, the pain instantly left me; and I felt strength flowing into my body. It looked like my miracle had finally come; but after the service, the pain returned worse than ever. It lingered day after day, and I eventually let that pain take the place of God's prophecy. In fact, I forgot about the prophecy altogether; and when you forget what God tells you, you're headed for trouble.

The Lord told me that all the light of Heaven is in each one of His prophecies, but I had let the light go out of His prophecy for me. My body was in an awful condition, and I was suffering death; it seemed like I couldn't live, and I couldn't die. My eyes were sunken way back into my head, and the grave appeared to be opening up before me because I had closed the Lord's door to my miracle when I had failed to remember His prophecy. I felt like I was in a room with no windows or doors, and I couldn't find my way out. God was healing others I had prayed for; but this was before I had received any of the gifts of the Spirit, and it seemed that He wasn't going to heal me.

My wife, Angel, loved me so much that she would spend many nights sitting on the floor praying and weeping as I suffered. I was so weak that she had to help me get dressed for the services; then I'd go into the pulpit and hold onto the Bible stand, trying not to show my pain—but God was there. When I would ask Him to help me, His power would come upon me and give me the strength to move about on the platform and deliver His message. Then souls would come to the altar to be saved, delivered, healed and blessed. I was determined to preach and do the Lord's work until I took my last breath because I loved the Gospel. If God wasn't going to heal me, I was determined to die in the pulpit…but I didn't want to die. I wanted to carry the Gospel of Jesus Christ to people all over the world.

JESUS MADE ME WHOLE

I couldn't understand why God wouldn't heal me. I knew He had called me and gifted me to preach at eighteen, and I loved preaching so much. I knew I had not committed one sin or disobedience since the day the Lord had saved me, so it just didn't make sense. But

what I didn't know at the time was that I had
to go through all of my suffering so the Lord
could make me into a vessel that He could use
with the nine gifts of the Spirit.

Then one night, Jesus came; and He made
me whole all over. His mighty power went
through me, and I couldn't even stand on my
feet. I had never felt such power from God
before, not even when I was baptized in the
Holy Ghost; and I knew right then that every
disease in my body had to have died. I knew
the Lord had made me whole, and I had no
trouble believing that because I had nothing
but pure faith. Suddenly, none of my tomorrows mattered; I knew God had healed me
and that I would be a greater testimony to
people than ever before. I would be able to
cry without one doubt, "You can be healed;
it's God's will for you to be healed!"

My healing was real, and I found that Jesus
was all He had claimed to be—He was truly
the healing Christ. I found that He had life
and the light to dispel all my darkness. I
saw Him with His love handkerchief that
wipes away all of our tears, and He gave me

a brand-new life so I could take the Gospel to the world.

CLAIM YOUR MIRACLE

After that night, the devil would try to talk to me saying, "You had better not say you're healed because you might not be"; but I didn't listen to him. Instead, I said, "Lord, I'm going to tell everyone I'm healed; and if I die, you'll be embarrassed." That may not sound right to you, but I was talking through faith. I had remembered the prophecy of my healing, and I knew God wasn't going to let me die because He had promised I was going to live. There were times when the pain would come back, but I was determined to die saying I was healed because there was no turning back for me.

I didn't doubt my miracle one bit. Throughout my illness, I had already fought doubt and fear like they were wild animals; but because of that, I've been able to help many people fight for what they have needed down through the years. I encourage people who have waited so long for a miracle because I know they're getting closer and closer every day without realizing it. What if I had given up before I made the last step that took me to victory? I would have missed stepping into life like I'd never experienced it before. I would have missed being healed all over!

That miracle still lives in me today; and many times as I'm lying in bed, I'll say, "I thank you for my miracle, Lord. I don't even have a pain all because of you!" God has given me good health these many years, and now I realize why I had to go into that valley of pain and sorrow. God was preparing me to feel the sorrows, heartaches and pains of other people so I would have great compassion for them. I don't give up on people unless God tells me that He's going to take a child of God home. At different times, He'll let me know that; and then I stop praying for that person's healing and instead ask God to take the person home without letting him or her suffer any longer.

GOD GAVE ME HIS GIFTS

When the Lord visited with me that miracle night, He lingered to tell me that He was going to use me in the healing ministry; and

I believed every word He said. Then He continued, "Later, you'll go on a long fast; and when you come off that fast, you'll have my power for the healing of the people." I had never counted myself worthy of having any of the nine gifts of the Spirit, and I knew that having them would require me to pay such a great price; but the Lord is the One who divides the gifts, and He's the One who chose me. That humbled me so much, and the Lord took me over with His love and humility.

He sent me into a revival for six weeks, and His mighty power fell! When we closed that revival, God led me into the fast He had told me about; and it changed my life completely. When the fast was over, I was very weak and lying on the couch when Angel leaned over me and asked, "Honey, do you have that power?" I said, "Yes, I have it." I didn't feel it at that time, but God had said it; I believed it, and that settled it.

Shortly after that, Angel and I headed for a revival at another minister's church; but I didn't tell him that I would be bringing the Jesus healing ministry. I wanted him to see it for himself, and God did move like I had never seen Him move before.

Some people love to boast that they have one of the nine gifts of the Spirit; but if the Lord gives someone one of His gifts, that person won't have to tell others about it. It will manifest itself in his or her life. Anyone who is born new and has the Holy Ghost can have the nine fruits of the Spirit, but God only gives His nine gifts to certain chosen ones.

Later, the Lord gave me the gift of discerning; and He told me that it was the most fragile of all the gifts. He instructed me not to discuss it with any other preacher because He said that I would be taught by the Holy Ghost. Today, I still depend totally on the Holy Spirit for direction in every service and for the use of each gift in my life.

HEALING POWER

The Holy Bible clearly states that healing comes from the Lord through His divine blood. **But he was wounded for our transgressions, he was bruised for our iniquities: the chastisement of our peace was upon him; and with his stripes we are healed**

(Isaiah 53:5). I believe in the power of prayer and in divine healing, and I know that healing only comes through the body of our Lord and Savior, Jesus Christ.

Some preachers actually fake miracles, and we've seen the results of such deceit when we travel to different nations. We hear about preachers who claim to bring miracles, but the miracles never last. Then we bring the people the truth—that miracles from the true and living God do last if those who receive them will live holy and treat God right.

Only God can heal; however, He has put a certain amount of healing in nature. If you cut yourself, the natural healing in your body will take care of that cut without your even having to pray about it; but if infection sets in, you have to seek additional help. God has given great knowledge to humanity that has enabled the medical field to take the healing He placed in nature and apply it to our bodies. I believe that God has given us good medicines to help in the healing of our bodies; and He obviously believes in good medicine or He wouldn't have said, **A merry heart doeth**

good like a medicine (Proverbs 17:22). God has instructed us to give honor where honor is due, and I want to pay tribute to all the fine doctors and nurses who are truly dedicated to helping the sick and afflicted. There are many medical people who support my worldwide ministry, and the power of God in this ministry is affecting doctors around the world. Their curiosity is stirred when they hear about hopeless cases being healed.

The greatest of all healing is the divine healing that was in Eden. Adam and Eve had that divine healing in their bodies; and since Jesus came, we who are born new have the divine Healer, the Master of all sicknesses and diseases. We don't have to look for the Lord because He's on duty for us all the time through the power of the Holy Ghost.

Medical science doesn't have the cure for everything. They have spent billions of dollars on research, but they still can't find the cure for cancer. It's heartbreaking to see people dying with such a horrible disease when you know the Lord can heal it as if it were just a slight headache.

Thousands of people have been healed of all types of cancer through this Jesus ministry, and God lets me see the cancer melting away through the power of His miracle star.

GOD HAS THE CURE FOR EVERYTHING

In one of my first tent meetings, a woman with a cancer the size of a quarter on her face came for prayer. As she started to leave the platform, the cancer fell off. She came rushing back to show me, and the spot where it had been didn't even look raw. I've never forgotten that miracle!

One of my uncles who had cancer on his face came to a North Carolina crusade for prayer. Early the next week, the cancer fell out in his hand when he was shaving. That meant so much to him and to me, and I was no doubt the instrument the Lord used to also win his soul.

If the first man and woman had obeyed God, the devil would have been destroyed thousands of years ago; and he never would have been able to afflict people. He would have been thrown into the lake of fire with all of his demonic spirits and the fallen angels, and this

Earth would have been Paradise. There would be no sickness, no death and no cemeteries; but instead, this world becomes more like hell every day. That's why Jesus came—to bring salvation and deliverance for all.

The soul will live forever either in Heaven or hell, but the human body has a death sentence upon it. **It is appointed unto men once to die** (Hebrews 9:27). We all have that sentence, but the Lord tells us that the sentence will be lifted when the Rapture takes place. **Behold, I shew you a mystery; We shall not all sleep, but we shall all be changed, In a moment, in the twinkling of an eye, at the last trump: for the trumpet shall sound, and the dead shall be raised incorruptible, and we shall be changed** (I Corinthians 15:51,52). We will vanish into thin air in our glorified bodies; but until that time, all must die.

That doesn't mean you should just give up when doctors can no longer help you. Man is not the final authority; God is. Look to Him knowing that through His love and companionship, He can heal you.

When a doctor tells someone that they're

going to die, that just causes me to use perfect faith through the blood for them; and that's why God can use me, His humble instrument, like He does. Jesus said, **The things which are impossible with men are possible with God** (Luke 18:27). Your case is possible with God no matter what the doctors have said. You have to learn to yield to your miracle because if you don't yield to one miracle, you're not likely to get others that you may need.

People that doctors have given up on will come to me for prayer, and many times they're some of the easiest people to pray for because they're focused completely upon Jesus; they know that the Lord is their only hope. Never tell a child of God that they're going to die. We're not supposed to help people get ready to die; we should be helping them get ready to be made whole and live.

LET JESUS BE REAL

The Holy Ghost is always teaching me more about Jesus and His ways. I depend on God, and I stay plugged into Heaven. Jesus came and put up a blood-line that enables us to call Heaven any time. The line is clear all the way from Earth to the throne of God, and it's there for all God's saints to use; the devil can't put any static on that line. When we encounter any static, it has to be coming from us because there isn't any in Heaven. When I don't get an answer from God or He doesn't plainly verify something to me, I want to know what's wrong. I want to be perfect in God's love and grace. I want to hear what His Spirit is saying in perfection, and I want to have clear eyes to see His manifestations.

Let the Lord be real to you, and that reality will give you strength. He is so real to me, and I'm so full of God's grace and power that the Holy Spirit can direct me in how to be just like Jesus. Of course, that doesn't mean I never get tired because the Bible tells us that even Jesus got tired. **Jesus therefore, being wearied with his journey, sat thus on the well** (John 4:6). At that time, I'm sure Jesus had been through much and hadn't had enough food or rest.

Think about how tired Jesus must have been when He would stay awake and talk to His Father at night while the disciples slept. Jesus would have liked for them to stay awake with Him, but they didn't. He even told them that His Father was their Father, but they didn't come into the reality of it until after they had received the Holy Ghost. It takes the Holy Ghost to make God and His Son as real to you as they should be.

The Bible says, **For I am the LORD, I change not** (Malachi 3:6). It also says, **Jesus Christ the same yesterday, and today, and forever** (Hebrews 13:8). I have had people actually request for me to ask God to change His mind, but that's ridiculous! I'll never ask the great God of the universe to change His mind about anything.

KEEP YOUR FIRST LOVE

You have to prepare for a miracle. How?— Go back to your first love. First love is what brought Jesus from Heaven and caused the Father to give His whole heart to us when His Son died on the Cross. **For God so loved the world, that he gave his only begotten Son, that whosoever believeth in him should not perish, but have everlasting life** (John 3:16). The Lord told me that when He made

Calvary, it was the first and only time He had ever used all of His love; and that love made it possible for us to have a blood-washed soul, a blood-washed heart and a blood-washed body. Jesus heals through love.

I have yielded to the great miracle that God gave me for many years, and it still gives me such strength and health today. It lives inside of me, and it keeps the love and the faith of God moving within. When trials come my way, I know without a doubt that both of my hands are in His. I know **that all things work together for good to them that love God, to them who are the called according to his purpose** (Romans 8:28). I fit right into that scripture, so I don't have to worry about anything. I know I won't die until the Lord wants me to; but if it's His will, I want to make it to Rapture Day.

The Lord actually gave me a vision of the Rapture, and it was a glorious experience that I've never forgotten. There were people all around me looking up and shouting, "Hallelujah, hallelujah!" It was so real that when I came to myself, I was also shouting,

"Hallelujah!" It was a great time.

Thou shalt love the Lord thy God with all thy heart, and with all thy soul, and with all thy mind, and with all thy strength: this is the first commandment (Mark 12:30). You must get back to your first love. It's the perfect place for you and will put you on the perfect road the Lord has planned for you. Is God really first in your life or does He have an accusation against you today? Leaving your first love is the first step toward backsliding because you will become lukewarm. First love sets you on fire with the Word of God. Heaven's great fire takes all the dross out and purifies you so you become like pure gold.

LIVING EPISTLES

Jesus said in the Sermon on the Mount, **Be ye therefore perfect, even as your Father which is in heaven is perfect** (Matthew 5:48). Only divinity can make us into that perfect, new creation. You may not always be perfect in the eyes of people, but you can be perfect in the eyes of God—perfect in His love and in His faith.

When I received salvation, God saved me through and through and made me perfect in Him. He changed me so completely that I had to get acquainted with the new me. All of a sudden, I felt as holy as if I was already in Heaven. I was so full of God and the reality of His power that I wanted to be with Him more than I wanted to eat, sleep or socialize with people. For the first six weeks after I had been saved, Jesus was always waiting at my door no matter what time it was. Whenever I'd go into my little bedroom and close the door, the Holy Spirit would take me over; and I loved it.

Shortly after that, the Lord started preaching through me; and His messages would roll forth like mighty waters. I loved preaching, and I was always dining in God's presence so that I would have good things to serve the people.

How much time do you actually spend in God's garden of love? Do you look forward to being alone with Him? Restlessness is of the world, and you can't always be running around here and there. You have to take time to be alone with God and His Word. How much do you treasure the Word? Only the Word can keep you from sin. **Thy word have I hid in mine heart, that I might not sin against thee** (Psalm 119:11). You have to hide the Word in your heart so it can keep you from sin, and you must also allow it to direct you. **O LORD, I know that the way of man is not in himself: it is not in man that walketh to direct his steps** (Jeremiah 10:23).

Do you have enough of the Word in you that it can make you a living epistle as the Bible declares you should be? **Forasmuch as ye are manifestly declared to be the epistle of Christ ministered by us, written not with ink, but with the Spirit of the living God; not in tables of stone, but in fleshy tables of the heart** (II Corinthians 3:3). Are you so full of the Spirit of God that you walk and talk just like this Bible says you should? Do you work for your Lord? Jesus said, **I must work the works of him that sent me, while it is day: the night cometh, when no man can work** (John 9:4). You must move on for the Lord because the hour is late!

The Lord let me know that you're wasting His precious, divine blood when you don't consistently pray, fast and live in the Word. The blood is overcoming power from Heaven, and the devil can't defeat that power. **But ye shall receive power, after that the Holy Ghost is come upon you** (Acts 1:8). Without this power, you won't be able to keep going with the Lord. You'll stray, and the little foxes will spoil the vine. **Take us the foxes, the little foxes, that spoil the vines: for our vines have tender grapes** (Song of Solomon 2:15). Big foxes can reach up and get the grapes; but little foxes can't do that, so they gnaw at the roots of the vine and kill the vine.

What is your condition today? You must hear the voice of the Lord calling, "Where art thou? I left my home in Heaven and went to Calvary just for you." What a price He paid!

ACCEPT GOD'S WAY

Are you bold with your testimonies of salvation and healing? Healing from Heaven is not make-believe; it's living reality. People will come to one of my services for prayer, and they have their whole healing process planned out in their minds; but when things don't go exactly their way, they'll leave angry. They act just like Naaman the captain of the Syrian army did when Elisha told him to go and dip in Jordan seven times. **So Naaman** [a leper] **came with his horses and with his chariot, and stood at the door of the house of Elisha. And Elisha sent a messenger unto him, saying, Go and wash in Jordan seven times, and thy flesh shall come again to thee, and thou shalt be clean** (II Kings 5:9,10).

That was not what Naaman had in mind; and he said, **Behold, I thought, He will surely come out to me, and stand, and call on the name of the LORD his God, and strike his hand over the place, and recover the leper. Are not Abana and Pharpar, rivers of Damascus, better than all the waters of Israel? may I not wash in them, and be clean? So he turned and went away in a rage** (II Kings 5:11,12). Elisha had insulted Naaman and made him angry. Naaman didn't want to go to Jordan because the Syrians hated that river. It reminded them of Jehovah God, and they didn't believe in Him. Naaman wasn't in any shape to be healed, and he didn't know that salvation and deliverance were waiting for him in that river.

Then one of his servants stepped up and said, **My father, if the prophet had bid thee do some great thing, wouldest thou not have done it? how much rather then, when he saith to thee, Wash, and be clean? Then went he down, and dipped himself seven times in Jordan, according to the saying of the man of God: and his flesh came again like unto the flesh of a little child, and he was clean** (II Kings 5:13,14). Thank God that Naaman listened to the servant and decided to go to Jordan. Each time he went down into the water, he felt a little better; and as promised, with the last dip he was made completely whole. Legions of devils couldn't have stopped him from rejoicing, and nothing could have made him doubt his miracle.

Naaman's great deliverance was also mentioned in the New Testament. **And many lepers were in Israel in the time of Eliseus the**

prophet; and none of them was cleansed, saving Naaman the Syrian (Luke 4:27). The Lord is still healing leprosy today, and I have received a testimony of four lepers being cleansed by the blest cloth. That's a wonderful testimony for the Lord and for this Jesus ministry.

Don't ever blame God for not answering your prayers because when He gets ready to move, He will. Just make sure all of your prayers are righteous and holy and that you pray them through the blood. The fact that God hears you must be a reality to you. It pleases God when we have enough faith to wait upon Him because as we wait, He works within us to furnish everything we need.

CHAPTER 2

Different Methods of Divine Healing

This chapter lists and explains God's different methods of healing. Many people think that God always works in the same way, but you must be aware that the Lord's healing can come in various ways.

NUMBER ONE:
THE PRAYER OF FAITH
AND ANOINTING WITH OIL

This method is brought to light in James. **Is any among you afflicted? let him pray** (James 5:13). You should always begin by praying for yourself. My mother prayed for herself before she would ever ask anybody else to pray for her, and her prayers always got through to Heaven. She wasn't continually asking the preacher to pray for her; and when she did need a preacher's prayers, we knew she was really sick.

Mama taught me that every time you prayed for yourself and got your answer, it would give you more faith and confidence in your own prayers. Whenever I would start to come down with something, she'd say, "Honey, you'd better get up your faith because the devil is going to try you." I've never heard anybody else use that phrase, but Mama believed that with her whole heart. Mama wanted people to get ready for miracles, and her way worked because it was God's way.

Today, I still pray for myself before I ever think about asking anybody else to pray for me because I know in whom I have believed. I know God will keep all I have committed into His hands and that He has the power to make me whole. You need to learn to pray for yourself, too; and if you're living holy, you should have more confidence in your prayers than you do in anybody else's prayers.

Is any merry? let him sing psalms (James 5:13). This refers to holy songs. Singing praises to the Lord will prepare you to believe and receive.

THE OIL OF THE SPIRIT

Is any sick among you? let him call for the elders of the church; and let them pray over him, anointing him with oil in the name of the Lord (James 5:14). The people referred to here are those who are full of the Holy Ghost and full of the love, power, peace and faith of God.

In Bible times, the elders of the church would anoint the sick with oil. These elders were men who were seasoned in the Lord, those who had spent time with the Lord and were not new to His ways. They knew how to inject the Holy Spirit, and the oil is a symbol of the Holy Spirit throughout the Word of God.

The Old Testament speaks much about the oil, and it was used as a point of contact. **And he arose, and went into the house; and he poured the oil on his head, and said unto**

him, Thus saith the LORD God of Israel, I
have anointed thee king over the people of
the LORD, even over Israel (II Kings 9:6).

In the New Testament, the parable of the ten
virgins tells us that the wise had the oil. **Then
shall the kingdom of heaven be likened
unto ten virgins, which took their lamps,
and went forth to meet the bridegroom.
And five of them were wise, and five were
foolish. They that were foolish took their
lamps, and took no oil with them: But the
wise took oil in their vessels with their
lamps** (Matthew 25:1–4).

When you pray for friends or loved ones,
you can anoint with oil; it's a Biblical method
of healing. My mother always anointed us
with oil, and she had great success with her
prayers. When you use a true method of God,
it puts you in touch with Him right away; you
don't have to struggle and fight to find Him.
Whenever Mama was called out to pray for
someone, she always took her bottle of oil.
Then she would come back looking so angelic
because God had brought victory.

I used olive oil until the Lord gave me His

gifts; then He let me know that I no longer needed to use oil because His gifts would be the point of contact. Most people do not have the gifts of the Spirit; but true children of God can anoint with oil and pray in faith believing, and people will be healed. Faith turns on the healing power of God. When you anoint an obedient heart, the power of God delivers; and that heart receives. We are to pass on what the Lord gives us and not hide any of God's greatness. I pass it on to everybody who will accept it and yield to it.

And the prayer of faith shall save the sick, and the Lord shall raise him up (James 5:15). The Lord clearly promised healing through prayer; and He went on to say, **and if he have committed sins, they shall be forgiven him** (James 5:15). When a person gets healed, God doesn't just heal the physical body; He heals the body and the spirit all at one time if the person will believe and accept it.

Pray one for another, that ye may be healed. The effectual fervent prayer of a righteous man availeth much (James 5:16).

The word "effectual" means prayers that are effective. The prayer of faith and the power of the Holy Spirit are effective and bring victory!

NUMBER TWO:
THE LAYING ON OF HANDS

Jesus said, **These signs shall follow them that believe...they shall lay hands on the sick, and they shall recover** (Mark 16:17,18). Notice that these signs shall follow believers, not doubters. These believers are Jesus believers—people who believe all that He taught and brought. Some people will get hands laid on them, but they don't really believe that they're going to get well. They just want to get a touch, so that's all they get. They don't claim their miracle and expect to be healed. I have had people come into my healing line again and again who would have been shocked if they had actually received anything because they didn't really believe.

The enemy tries to make people believe that God doesn't want to heal them or that they didn't really receive their miracle. Some people will come for prayer, and the Lord will let me know that they're healed; but they won't hold on to it, and they'll let doubt creep in. Others are satisfied with being slain in the Spirit. *They just want to feel the Spirit; but they don't come expecting to be healed, saith the Lord.* When I need a miracle, I don't only want a touch; I want the miracle. When God touches you, you have to decide that from the very moment you're touched by a believer, you're going to get well. You have to claim your promise.

Some people think that the more often they have hands laid on them, the quicker they'll get healed; but God doesn't always work that way. It's all right to have hands laid on you more than once, but to make a habit of it shows that you're not yielding to the Holy Spirit.

When you take a pill for something, do you assume that the pill isn't any good if it doesn't suddenly make you well? No, you continue taking the medication as prescribed by your doctor. How much more should we follow God's instructions? They're in the Bible for all believers to read and follow; but you have to be a believer who lives a holy life, and then you can expect healing from Heaven.

Consider the woman in the Bible who was bent over and couldn't raise herself up for eighteen years. **And, behold, there was a woman which had a spirit of infirmity eighteen years, and was bowed together, and could in no wise lift up herself. And when Jesus saw her, he called her to him, and said unto her, Woman, thou art loosed from thine infirmity. And he laid his hands on her: and immediately she was made straight, and glorified God** (Luke 13:11–13). Jesus laid His hands on that woman, and immediately she could stand up straight after eighteen years. He could have healed her without laying hands on her, but He was teaching us this healing method. The woman then glorified and honored God, and that's why she got her miracle.

UNBELIEF IS DESTRUCTIVE

It's sad that the scribes and Pharisees didn't believe in God or honor Him for His miracles. They even complained about the woman with arthritis being healed on the Sabbath; but

Jesus said, **Ought not this woman, being a daughter of Abraham, whom Satan hath bound, lo, these eighteen years, be loosed from this bond on the sabbath day** (Luke 13:16)? Today, many preachers and teachers still don't believe in miracles, and some actually believe that sickness comes from God. The devil loves to do his dirty work and then make people think that God did it; but when you do away with God's miracles, you've done away with God.

When I first received the gift of discerning, a woman came before me in a great crusade, and she didn't believe God loved her. I wanted to know why; and as she stood before me, God took me into a vision. I saw the girl's mother lying in bed; and the girl, who looked to be about five years old at the time, was standing by crying. I also saw a man of the cloth standing there, and he was telling the little girl that it was God's will for her mother to be dying of cancer. At that moment, the young girl had turned her back on God because she didn't want any part of a God who would take her mother like that.

She had carried that bitterness up until the time that I met her as a grown woman.

At that service, I told the woman what I had seen in the vision and explained that the so-called man of God wasn't a man of God at all and that he had lied to her. She knew that I didn't know anything about her or her mother, so I had her attention. Her hard, outer crust started to crack, and her tears began to flow. She melted before the presence of God, and He gloriously saved her soul. The Lord's power, love and grace came upon her in a great way; and they swept all her bitterness away. She had come into a brand-new world in a moment of time, and she was lit up with the glory of the Lord.

The devil had bound that woman with that lie for all those years. It's awful that a supposed servant of God would do such a thing to a child. She thought God had robbed her of her mother, but the true and living God set her free; and I have always remembered her glorious conversion.

NUMBER THREE:
THE TRUTH IN THE SPOKEN WORD

And ye shall know the truth, and the truth shall make you free (John 8:32). The only way you can be truly free is by knowing the truth about yourself, but that's the last person some of you will ever realize the truth about because you won't accept it. You'll believe the truth about others, but the devil robs you when it comes to learning about yourself. *That's why some of you don't have more blessings, saith the Lord.*

Come into the truth of God and then live there. There's plenty of room for all people throughout the whole Earth; but today, most people have trampled on God's truth. **Judgment is turned away backward, and justice standeth afar off: for truth is fallen in the street, and equity cannot enter** (Isaiah 59:14). How many people really love the truth and will accept all of it?—very few.

The Word of truth heals. **He sent his word, and healed them** (Psalm 107:20). Jesus was the Word made flesh. **And the Word was made flesh, and dwelt among us, (and we**

beheld his glory, the glory as of the only begotten of the Father,) full of grace and truth (John 1:14). Jesus came to heal and deliver people. **They brought unto him many that were possessed with devils: and he cast out the spirits with his word, and healed all that were sick** (Matthew 8:16). Notice that the Word of God will cast out any devils, and the Bible tells us that every word was given with power. **And they were astonished at his doctrine: for his word was with power** (Luke 4:32).

When you look in the Bible, you'll notice that wherever Jesus went, there were miracles and healings. He even raised the dead. Lazarus had been dead for four days, but Jesus raised him up just as if he had suffered only a slight headache. The blood and the Word will do the same thing for people today, and I impart that blood through faith into each person who comes to me for prayer.

BELIEVE THE WORD

The Syrophenician woman wasn't even of the household of faith, but she knew about and believed in Jesus, the Word. Her daughter was devil possessed, and there was nothing she could do for her; so she went to find Jesus. **Then came she and worshipped him, saying, Lord, help me. But he answered and said, It is not meet to take the children's bread, and to cast it to dogs. And she said, Truth, Lord: yet the dogs eat of the crumbs which fall from their masters' table. Then Jesus answered and said unto her, O woman, great is thy faith: be it unto thee even as thou wilt. And her daughter was made whole from that very hour** (Matthew 15:25–28).

When I read of the woman saying, "Even the dogs eat the crumbs that fall from their master's table," that makes me want to weep because she had such humility. Are you humble enough for the Lord to tell you what's hindering you if you're having trouble receiving? The Lord told this humble woman that the devils had departed from her daughter; the Word spoke, and she believed. Some of you would have stayed and begged; and if this woman would have done that, then Jesus would have had to say, "I already told you that your daughter is delivered." But He didn't have to say that to her. Jesus spoke, and it was done.

A rich nobleman's son was dying, and the man went to Jesus looking for a miracle. The man thought Jesus would have to go to his son, but the Lord just spoke the words. **Jesus saith unto him, Go thy way; thy son liveth. And the man believed the word that Jesus had spoken unto him, and he went his way. And as he was now going down, his servants met him, and told him, saying, Thy son liveth. Then inquired he of them the hour when he began to amend. And they said unto him, Yesterday at the seventh hour the fever left him. So the father knew that it was at the same hour, in the which Jesus said unto him, Thy son liveth: and himself believed, and his whole house** (John 4:50–53). The nobleman used faith in the presence of the Lord, and his son was made whole.

The Word makes all the difference. It came to Earth in a body of flesh; and if you're holy like the Lord, the divine Word will work for you and through you just like it did when Jesus was here. When you speak, the devils will have to go out of people; and diseases will have to flee or melt away.

NUMBER FOUR:
THE ANOINTED CLOTH

People are being healed all over the world through the blest cloths. **And God wrought special miracles by the hands of Paul: So that from his body were brought unto the sick handkerchiefs or aprons, and the diseases departed from them, and the evil spirits went out of them** (Acts 19:11,12). Aprons or handkerchiefs were sent out from the body of Paul, not because his human body was anything great but because it was holy. The Holy Ghost dwelled within him, and he had the nine gifts of the Spirit. The Holy Ghost could use those gifts through him at any time because he was obedient to God.

Notice that the verse states "special miracles." Through the blest cloth, you can have any special miracle you need; and this ministry sends those cloths all over the world. The Lord creates and re-creates; and the blest cloth carries all the anointing you need to break every yoke, whether it's spiritual, physical or financial. **And it shall come to pass in that day, that his burden shall be taken away from off thy shoulder, and his yoke from off thy neck, and the yoke shall be destroyed because of the anointing** (Isaiah 10:27). That anointing is a blood anointing, or it wouldn't do the work.

You have to depend on God's anointings. Many of you believe in bathing before you start your day, but you don't think about taking an anointing from God so you can be free of all the yokes and bondages of the devil.

NUMBER FIVE:
TOUCHING THE HEM OF HIS GARMENT

And whithersoever he entered, into villages, or cities, or country, they laid the sick in the streets, and besought him that they might touch if it were but the border of his garment: and as many as touched him were made whole (Mark 6:56). These people wanted a touch of deliverance from Jesus, and as many as touched the hem of His garment and believed were healed.

By faith, you can touch Jesus at any time for anything you need when you're walking in the divine will of God. If you're yielding to the Lord, walking in the steps of Jesus and seeking with your whole heart to be just like Him, you'll get answers.

The woman with the issue of blood touched Jesus and believed. **And a woman having an issue of blood twelve years, which had spent all her living upon physicians, neither could be healed of any, Came behind him, and touched the border of his garment: and immediately her issue of blood stanched** (Luke 8:43,44). It appears that the woman had been very wealthy because the Bible says that she had spent all her living and was no better. But she said, **If I may but touch his garment, I shall be whole** (Matthew 9:21). She didn't have to have everything her way; she didn't have to talk to Jesus for a half hour or so, and she didn't ask Him to pray for her. She talked faith to herself; and when she was told that she couldn't get to Jesus, she didn't let it hinder her. She knew crowds of people would be swarming around such a man, but she just wanted to touch His garment.

As a child of God, you should be that close to Jesus all the time; but you have to use your faith. You have to go from faith to the hem of His garment, from faith to Jesus and from faith to His promises of healing.

NUMBER SIX:
THE WRITTEN WORD

We have the written Word. **It is written, Man shall not live by bread alone, but by every word that proceedeth out of the mouth of God** (Matthew 4:4). The Word declares that Jesus saves and heals. **And the people, when they knew it, followed him** [Jesus]**: and he received them, and spake unto them of the kingdom of God, and healed them that had need of healing** (Luke 9:11). Everything we need has been written in the Bible, and you must know God's Word so well that you can feed it to the devil. Jesus gives us the authority to use the Word, but you can't use it unless you study it. **Study to shew thyself approved unto God, a workman that needeth not to be ashamed, rightly dividing the word of**

truth (II Timothy 2:15).

People may brag about how many times they've read through the Bible, but that doesn't mean anything to me. I want to know how much of the Bible they have studied and applied to their lives. How real have God and His works become to them? How much of the Word have they hidden in their hearts? Proverbs says it will bring healing to our flesh. **My son, attend to my words; incline thine ear unto my sayings. Let them not depart from thine eyes; keep them in the midst of thine heart. For they are life unto those that find them, and health to all their flesh** (Proverbs 4:20–22). Get ready for your miracle. It doesn't matter what you need; the Lord said that you can be cured right here in His Word.

The truth in the written Word brings faith. **So then faith cometh by hearing, and hearing by the word of God** (Romans 10:17). Divine faith is doing exactly what God tells you to do. You can't just ask the Lord to give you faith; you have to believe for it. If you need more faith, just pray, **Lord, I believe;**

help thou mine unbelief (Mark 9:24). Sometimes, the Lord makes us wait on purpose because He's waiting for just the right time to move.

Every Word of God has healing in it, and Jesus came and brought that healing to everyone who will accept it. It's not magic; it comes through divine love, and love is our great healing balm. You can't buy it with money; you can only get it through humility and obedience. However, you have to continue to be obedient if you want to keep it.

NUMBER SEVEN:
THE COVENANT OF AGREEMENT

If two of you shall agree on earth as touching anything that they shall ask, it shall be done for them of my Father which is in heaven (Matthew 18:19). Don't ask just anybody to agree with you; choose someone who has the faith of God, is obedient to Him and is walking in the footsteps of Jesus.

I try to get people who come into the prayer line to agree with me for their miracles; but at times, I just have to move on because some aren't there to agree but just to see. Some people carry a critical spirit within while others claim that they're saved when they're not. When they make false claims, it's just the voice of the devil speaking through them; and it sends cold chills through me. It makes some people angry when I tell them they're not saved, and they'll leave cursing God; but just think what it will be like when they wake up in hell. If they remain deceived on this Earth, they'll change their minds in eternity.

CHAPTER 3

The Spirit of Believing and Receiving

*M*iracles are God's divine plan for the Bride, but we must stay yielded to divinity in order to receive. The healing power from Heaven brings all the miracles and healings we will ever need and all the direction we must have for our lives. The whole will of God comes in healing from Heaven; but there is so much that has to be done within each one of us before we are qualified to receive everything that the Lord wants to serve us for our bodies, minds, souls and spirits. The mission of the Holy Ghost is to teach us divinity and to guide us in all God's ways of truth.

Children of God must walk in the Spirit every day or the old Adamic nature that was once buried will take them over again, and they will fall into the hands of the devil just like Adam and Eve did. The Lord wants you to always be aware that the spirit is willing, but the flesh is weak. **Watch and pray, that ye enter not into temptation: the spirit indeed is willing, but the flesh is weak** (Matthew 26:41).

BOW TO GOD'S WILL

Are you willing to do anything that the Lord wants you to do? I was willing to do anything for God if He would just heal me, and that's why He was able to make me whole. When Jesus was here, He always stayed in the will of the Father; and He was the perfect man. Even Pilate had to admit, **I find no fault in this man** (Luke 23:4).

In the Garden of Gethsemane when Jesus was suffering such pain and agony from carrying our sicknesses, diseases and sins, He bowed to His Father's will. In the human, Jesus said, **Father, if thou be willing, remove this cup from me.** But then He quickly went on to say, **Nevertheless not my will, but thine, be done** (Luke 22:42). Don't deceive yourself and tell the Lord that you want His will if you're not going to accept it, and don't ask Him for it if you're just going to grumble and complain about it. When you do that, you're in no shape to do God's will.

Jesus bowed to God's divine will, but then things got worse for Him instead of better. During His trial, He was kept up all night going from one judgment hall to another. The Roman soldiers beat Him almost to death, gave Him a Cross to carry and sent Him on His way to Calvary; but He had only a human body that was no stronger than yours or mine, and He fell beneath the load of the Cross. Somebody else had to carry the Cross for Him the rest of the way. **And as they led him away, they laid hold upon one Simon, a Cyrenian, coming out of the country, and on him they laid the cross, that he might bear it after Jesus** (Luke 23:26). Jesus followed behind as the soldiers continued to whip and beat Him the whole way.

Many people think that Jesus was only

beaten at the whipping post, but that's not so. The devil saw to it that He was beaten and spit upon all the way to Golgotha. Even when He was on the Cross and already in such agony, the soldiers continued to mock Him saying, **If thou be the king of the Jews, save thyself** (Luke 23:37).

Jesus knew that His death would give all mankind a chance at eternal life in Heaven. When He was here, He said, **And I, if I be lifted up from the earth, will draw all men unto me. This he said, signifying what death he should die** (John 12:32,33). Today, when we lift up Jesus as Savior, Lord and Master, He will draw people to us. He will also draw us to Himself daily in prayers, consecrations and at different times in fastings. We will be drawn to do the whole will of God, whatever it may be.

TAKE YOUR STAND

At Calvary, Jesus paid the blood price for every person to have all the healings, miracles and divinity needed; yet some go around carrying bags of depression, oppression and despair. They live so far beneath their privilege that it breaks my heart, and I know it grieves the Holy Spirit. When depression tries to close in on you, think about all of God's promises and claim them. Think about all the promises God has already fulfilled for you and all the miracles and healings you've received.

We must not only be filled with the truth but use it because we're in spiritual warfare. We have to be good soldiers just as Paul said. **Thou therefore endure hardness, as a good soldier of Jesus Christ** (II Timothy 2:3). Paul wanted Timothy to put on and keep on the whole armor of God. **Wherefore take unto you the whole armour of God, that ye may be able to withstand in the evil day, and having done all, to stand. Stand therefore, having your loins girt about with truth, and having on the breastplate of righteousness; And your feet shod with the preparation of the gospel of peace; Above all, taking the shield of faith, wherewith ye shall be able to quench all the fiery darts of the wicked. And take the helmet of salvation, and the sword of the Spirit, which is the word of**

God (Ephesians 6:13–17).

When you put on the whole armor of God, you can stand tall and command the devil to move out of the way. If you don't wear that armor today, you're in danger. You're supposed to stand as tall as Jesus, so you should always measure yourself with the true measuring rod—Jesus. **Till we all come in the unity of the faith, and of the knowledge of the Son of God, unto a perfect man, unto the measure of the stature of the fulness of Christ** (Ephesians 4:13). I always measure myself with Jesus to see if I'm like Him.

Don't let family, friends or co-workers affect your walk with the Lord. If they make fun of your fellowship with the Lord or mock His miracles and healings, stay away from them. Some of you think you have to be surrounded by unsaved family members who don't make you happy and ruin every holiday you spend with them. If any members of my family criticize God or what I preach, I don't want to have anything to do with them. I just put them under the blood and leave them there. If they don't yield to the blood, they'll lift up their eyes in hell one day; but I won't be responsible.   If my parents had acted like some people, I'd never have gone around them from the time I found God and was old enough to live on my own.

You don't have to have anybody but Jesus to make you happy.   Take Him as yours for the whole journey, and He'll stand by you in life or in death when you let Him have His way.   **As for God, his way is perfect** (Psalm 18:30).   Jesus showed us that if you don't let the Father have His will in everything, He can't do His perfect work.   If something is perfect, then there's nothing that needs to be changed or added to it; it's complete.   **Ye are complete in him, which is the head of all principality and power** (Colossians 2:10). Paul let us know that we are complete in Christ Jesus; there's no lack in Him.   We have all the divinity we need to walk the waters of life and God's seas of promises so He can do in our own individual lives all that He desires to do.

THE EARLY CHURCH USED DIVINITY

Take time to study the book of Acts. It's very deep; and in it, you'll find more divinity and more ways to receive from God than anywhere else. Divinity became so much the center of the Early Church members' lives that nothing could stop them. They didn't gather together to drink coffee and eat donuts; they went from house to house breaking the bread of Holy Communion in divine fellowship, and many people were healed and delivered. Later, the Early Church was persecuted, and its members were scattered everywhere; but they still continued to preach Jesus. **Therefore they that were scattered abroad went everywhere preaching the word** (Acts 8:4).

One day, when Peter and John were going up to the temple to pray, they passed by a man in his forties who had been crippled all of his life. **Now Peter and John went up together into the temple at the hour of prayer, being the ninth hour. And a certain man lame from his mother's womb was carried, whom they laid daily at the gate of the temple which is**

called Beautiful, to ask alms of them that entered into the temple; Who seeing Peter and John about to go into the temple asked an alms (Acts 3:1–3).

Peter and John had probably passed by that man many times before they had received the Holy Ghost, but they had not been ready for God to use them. However, after receiving the Holy Ghost, they had become strong in the Lord; and as Peter and John approached the temple, I'm sure the crippled man saw that their faces were shining. **And Peter, fastening his eyes upon him with John, said, Look on us. And he gave heed unto them, expecting to receive something of them** (Acts 3:4,5). Expectation means you expect to receive with no doubt, and that expectation helped the man to get ready for what was to come.

Peter looked at the man and said, **Silver and gold have I none; but such as I have give I thee: In the name of Jesus Christ of Nazareth rise up and walk** (Acts 3:6). Peter had the man's complete attention, and he used the name of Jesus to bring about a miracle.

And he [Peter] took him by the right hand, and lifted him up: and immediately his feet and ankle bones received strength. And he leaping up stood, and walked, and entered with them into the temple, walking, and leaping, and praising God (Acts 3:7,8).

Peter had no doubt that the man would be able to stand, so he reached out and grabbed him by the hand. The man had never walked in his life, but he didn't have to learn; he jumped up leaping and shouting. **And all the people saw him walking and praising God: And they knew that it was he which sat for alms at the Beautiful gate of the temple: and they were filled with wonder and amazement at that which had happened unto him** (Acts 3:9,10).

Peter and John didn't want any glory for the miracle, so they continued on their way; but the people went after them, wanting to know how this miracle had taken place. Peter finally stopped and said, **Ye men of Israel, why marvel ye at this? or why look ye so earnestly on us, as though by our own power or holiness we had made this man to walk?**

The God of Abraham, and of Isaac, and of Jacob, the God of our fathers, hath glorified his Son Jesus; whom ye delivered up, and denied him in the presence of Pilate, when he was determined to let him go. But ye denied the Holy One and the Just, and desired a murderer to be granted unto you; And killed the Prince of life, whom God hath raised from the dead; whereof we are witnesses. And his name through faith in his name hath made this man strong, whom ye see and know: yea, the faith which is by him hath given him this perfect soundness in the presence of you all (Acts 3:12–16).

Peter told the people exactly how the miracle had been done, and then he told them about Christ. **Neither is there salvation in any other: for there is none other name under heaven given among men, whereby we must be saved** [or healed] (Acts 4:12). Salvation includes healing, and there's no other name that can do these things.

GET RID OF DOUBT

In our overseas crusades, I call down miracles upon multitudes of people in the name of Jesus; and they receive by the thousands. Some will come to the crusades totally blind or deaf, and they receive their miracles as I call down the power of God on them.

When we were in the Dominican Republic for a crusade, a nice-looking young man brought his sister who was blind. I called sight to her eyes, and she instantly received her miracle. Her brother didn't believe it, so he asked her what color shirt and tie he was wearing. She immediately told him, and God shocked that brother. I hope he got rid of all of his doubt.

I make no room for doubt, but some of you do. The devil likes that little patch he has in your heart so why don't you get rid of him? Believe God and get well! I don't fight doubt; I use faith, and divine faith destroys doubt. I hate the devil, and I use my temper against him.

I had a furious temper when I was growing up; but everything changed when I got saved, and that convinced my family that I was definitely a born-new person. I no longer let anything bother me; I had it all under control through Jesus. Jesus didn't take my temper away; He just redirected it at the devil. That's why God can use me in such a great way to cast out devils—because I hate him with all the power of God within me. I can see what the devil has done and is still doing to human beings, and I fight back. God has made me a fighter.

DON'T BE DISCOURAGED

I don't allow discouragement in my spirit; that's one of the devil's greatest tools to use against people. He gets inside of them, and he grinds them down. He can take the very heart out of people; but you don't have to let that happen to you, especially since we have Calvary.

I learned years ago that when discouragement comes my way, I need to study the life of Noah. For 120 years, Noah took every opportunity to preach the truth; yet he wasn't able to get one soul saved because nobody wanted God. People were teaching their children against God just as they do today.

If you're discouraged, then you're not looking up to Jesus; and you're not expecting Him to come at any time. He said, **Be ye therefore ready also: for the Son of man cometh at an hour when ye think not** (Luke 12:40). Are you ready to get out of here? Let the Holy Spirit help you examine yourself with truth. Do you have a clear conscience before God? Are you honest and just? Do you have a true report when you talk to people, or is it a false one? Do you have God's love and divinity? Do you spend time thanking God for loving you? Where would you and I be without His love? We know it brought salvation to us so why should we ever doubt anything else that it brought?

I want you to consider God's love, and then I want you to think about hate. You can have one or the other, but you can't have both. Just as water and oil do not mix, neither do love and hate. Many so-called Christians who think they're full of love are actually deceived about themselves because they have hatred in their hearts.

God takes me right into people's souls, and I can see what's in them. When they're living for God, I will see a cross completely lit up;

but when they're failing God, just part of the cross lights up. If you could look into your soul today, what would you see? Would your cross be lit up? The Cross means everything to Heaven. When Jesus died for us, He took those black, dark, sinful crosses and made them glorious crosses of forgiveness, humility, hope, faith, love and peace that passes all understanding.

Through the Spirit of God, sinful, degraded souls can look like an old stump that worms have eaten all the life out of. God showed me a certain preacher's soul that looked like that; and later, all of his sins were uncovered. Another time, when I was conducting an out-of-state funeral, somebody introduced me to a pastor; and God let me know that the pastor didn't have any God in him at all. He was supposed to have been a Pentecostal pastor, but no Cross of Calvary lit up in his soul; and it makes me weep even now when I think about it. He's in the pulpit, but he has no God to feed his people.

ACT LIKE JESUS

I don't share with people everything the Lord reveals to me; I depend on the divine wisdom and knowledge of God to know how much to tell a person. Some people have asked me to tell them if I ever see anything wrong with them; but most of the time, they don't really mean it. One woman who thought she did mean it actually had a big mouth and a long tongue. She'd come to church and appear to be a saint; but she was always talking about people, and she argued with her husband all the time.

One day, she was cleaning one of the Sunday school rooms in my church; and I came across her as I was walking around and praying in the building. As soon as she saw me, she said, "Rev. Angley, I want you to tell me what's wrong with me." Without blinking an eye, I said, "Your mouth is too big." Well, that statement shocked her, but I didn't apologize because she had asked for it. Later, God got a hold of that woman's heart and led her on a forty-day fast. Afterward, she became a different person; and she's in Heaven today.

Do you act like Jesus, or are you deceived about yourself as this woman was? God loves everybody, but He certainly doesn't like some people; and I want God to like me. God's people should never argue and fight. It takes two people to have an argument; so if you have a companion who always wants to pick a fight, the best thing to do is not to react the same way in return. **Blessed are the peacemakers: for they shall be called the children of God** (Matthew 5:9). We must have no other seeds to sow but those of peace, grace, wisdom, love, faith and understanding.

WHAT'S IN YOUR SPIRIT?

Some people carry bitterness and malice toward others, even toward those in their own family. They may claim that they simply don't like certain people; but they had better admit that it's more than that because in some cases, it's actually hate.

You can't have both hate and love, and love has nothing to do with grudges and bitterness; they have to be part of the past. You can't be bitter toward anyone or even toward the way you were raised; you must know that your real life began when you were born new.

Grudges lead to pouting, and some people take offense at the smallest things. But God's Spirit doesn't pout; it lifts people up. Some people take on such a pouting spirit that they won't even speak to others in their own homes, but you'll never have any influence over anyone when you do that. If you shut yourself away to pout, you'll still be in that room pouting when the Rapture takes place. You'll hear people outside crying and screaming that their babies and small children are missing, and then you'll realize that you missed the most glorious event ever just because you wanted to pout. God can't stand it when people act so stupid.

Some may not have bitterness or hold grudges, but they talk too much. They like to tell others their whole life's history, but you should never trust anybody with your secrets. The minute they get upset with you, they'll tell a friend everything you've told them; then that friend will tell another friend, and so it goes. You shouldn't trust anyone but Jesus with all of your secrets. I share my whole heart with

Him because my heart belongs to Him. He said, **Blessed are the pure in heart: for they shall see God** (Matthew 5:8).

A VOICE OF LOVE

One of my favorite sayings is *no one has ever loved you like Jesus loves you; no one has ever cared for you like He cares.* Years ago, I would end my radio broadcasts with that statement; and I found out later that it changed lives. I met a man who had heard me preach on the radio, and he said that those words convicted him and brought him to the Lord. That miracle of salvation took place because I had shared Jesus' love with him.

Jesus loves us, and I never forget that even when I'm being persecuted. This ministry is persecuted because it's the Jesus ministry, but persecution is good for you if you don't become bitter. Down through the years, I'd think of myself as a big nail and persecution as a big sledgehammer. Every time the hammer would hit me, it would drive me deeper in the Lord. Your enemies can be your greatest blessings if you allow them to be; they'll make you fast, pray and lean more on Jesus.

We need Jesus' voice of love. Jesus was human, but His human voice had divinity in it; and He showed us that we could all have that presence in our voices, too. I have such great success on the mission fields because I live with God, and He uses my voice. The same authority is in my voice that Jesus used to raise Lazarus from the dead, but all the miracles are done by Him; God gets all the glory.

When soldiers came to arrest Jesus in the Garden of Gethsemane, Peter took matters into his own hands and used a sword to cut off a man's ear...and he was probably ready to cut the man's head off, too. But Jesus took the sword out of Peter's hand with His voice of love and told him, **Put up thy sword into the sheath: the cup which my Father hath given me, shall I not drink it** (John 18:11)?

What kind of love do you have? God's love doesn't cut off ears; it puts them back on and re-creates that which the devil has destroyed. The devil, on the other hand, has no love, only hate.

The Word ministry came to Earth in the form of a man with two eyes, two ears, two legs, two feet and two hands just like ours; and whatever the Word spoke came to pass. Remember that in the beginning, the Word of God spoke the stars, the moon and the sun into existence. **And God said, Let there be lights in the firmament of the heaven to divide the day from the night…And God made two great lights; the greater light to rule the day, and the lesser light to rule the night: he made the stars also** (Genesis 1:14,16). The grass, the fish and the birds were all created through the voice of divinity. **And God said, Let the waters bring forth abundantly the moving creature that hath life, and fowl that may fly above the earth in the open firmament of heaven** (Genesis 1:20). That voice has done and is still doing great things, and you have to have God's pure love before you can have that same voice.

LET DIVINITY DWELL WITHIN

You must use divinity and let divinity use you, but that can only be done in perfection through the Holy Spirit dwelling inside of you; He can't just be outside. You must be conscious of the fact that your body is the temple of the Holy Ghost, and it must be kept holy. **What? know ye not that your body is the temple of the Holy Ghost which is in you, which ye have of God, and ye are not your own** (I Corinthians 6:19)? The Holy Ghost is the One who leads you to Calvary in the first place so you can become a new creature, and then He begins to teach you divinity. If you have the real Holy Ghost, He's with you twenty-four hours a day; and He can heal you even while you're sleeping. How many times have you gotten up in the morning to find that you were no longer sick? The Lord let you sleep while the Holy Spirit did the work; and whether you realized it or not, you went to sleep in the blood.

God's works are miraculous works, and they all come through divinity. Don't expect your prayers to reach Heaven if they're not prayed through divinity because that's the only way you'll reach God. So many people who have God today don't do that; they're rich and don't know it. Life is not in possessions; real life can be found only in God. People may have diamonds and pearls, silver and gold, houses and lands; but if they don't have Jesus, they have nothing.

Before Jesus came to Earth, He was rich and living with His Father in Heaven; but He made Himself poor so that we could be rich in the things of God. **For ye know the grace of our Lord Jesus Christ, that, though he was rich, yet for your sakes he became poor, that ye through his poverty might be rich** (II Corinthians 8:9).

Some people are always seeking the golden calf, but I've never done that. Jesus is more precious to me than all the gold and silver in the world, and I trust Him for everything—do you? To trust Him means to love Him.

A BLESSING OR A CURSE?

If you really love God today, your life will glorify God; and your home will be a place of holiness. Parents, you are to be the head of your home, and you need to know what your children are doing. Do you know how they're using the computer in your home? *Thus saith the Lord, you must know.* Don't just ask them about it; you need to check it out yourself when they're not around. The Bible tells us, **Behold, I send you forth as sheep in the midst of wolves: be ye therefore wise as serpents, and harmless as doves** (Matthew 10:16).

Computers can be a great source of help and information, but they can also be an ungodly damnation in the hands of people who are not full of the Lord. Do you have enough God in your life to overcome the evil that is available through the computer? You may say that you just want to see what's on there, but quit lying to yourself and admit that you're lusting after unclean things. If you're always on there talking to all kinds of devil-possessed people, God is warning you today.

If you don't have enough of the grace of God to stay away from the evil that is available through the Internet, then you don't have enough grace to go to Heaven. You're unholy and ungodly, and you're thriving on filth instead of on divinity. God hates you like He did the Pharisees. **Woe unto you, scribes and Pharisees, hypocrites!...Ye serpents,**

ye generation of vipers, how can ye escape the damnation of hell (Matthew 23:29,33)? Being compared to a snake is about as low as you can go.

This lust spreads to dating, and many young people today can't keep their hands to themselves. If they had true salvation, they'd keep their hands holy; but some only pretend that they have divinity, when it's really just a counterfeit. God knows whether or not people have real salvation; and He's calling to them in great sorrow asking, "Where art thou?" If they don't heed, they'll be left when the Rapture takes place because the Lord is only coming for people who are without spot, wrinkle or blemish. **That he might present it to himself a glorious church, not having spot, or wrinkle, or any such thing; but that it should be holy and without blemish** (Ephesians 5:27).

You have to get every grain of sand out of the way and be rooted and grounded in Jesus Christ to be ready to get out of here. When the divine blood covers your soul, all Heaven can look upon it and see that you're pure, clean and holy. Jesus can say to you, **Thou art all fair, my love; there is no spot in thee** (Song of Solomon 4:7).

You may say that you can't stop yourself from doing the things you're doing, but it's because you don't want to. When the prodigal decided he wanted to go home, he said, **I will arise and go to my father, and will say unto him, Father, I have sinned against heaven, and before thee, And am no more worthy to be called thy son: make me as one of thy hired servants** (Luke 15:18,19). The son had finally humbled himself, and he asked if he could be just a servant; but when prodigal sons and daughters come home, all Heaven rejoices. The Father is always waiting, and Jesus is at the gate to welcome them.

YOU MUST NOT FAIL

If you're failing God today, Jesus is at your gate; but one day you'll be in eternity, and He won't be there any longer. Oh, how you'll wish then that He could be at the gate just one more time, but it will be too late. The only thing you'll hear is, **Depart from me, ye cursed, into everlasting fire, prepared for**

the devil and his angels (Matthew 25:41).
There are no winners at the devil's gambling
table. **For the wages of sin is death; but
the gift of God is eternal life through Jesus
Christ our Lord** (Romans 6:23). Jesus gave
His life for us. Don't trample His blood or
His love, grace, goodness and mercy under-
foot; or you'll go straight to hell.

God made hell for the devil and his angels,
but hell had to be enlarged to make room for
the human beings who are now going there,
too. **Therefore hell hath enlarged herself,
and opened her mouth without measure:
and their glory, and their multitude, and
their pomp, and he that rejoiceth, shall
descend into it** (Isaiah 5:14). How sad!

I thank God that my mother and dad didn't
believe the doctrine of "once in grace always
in grace" which says that you can't backslide
no matter what you do. The Bible teaches
against all sin, and my parents knew and
believed the Word. I often wonder how many
people have gone to hell thinking that they
were saved.

In today's world, you must have a passport if

you want to enter another country; and if you lose your passport, that country won't let you in no matter what you say. The same thing is true with your heavenly passport—if you sin, you'll lose it; and you'll never make it to Glory. The Bible says, **He that committeth sin is of the devil; for the devil sinneth from the beginning** (I John 3:8).

God is giving everyone a chance now, and He wants to give you everything He has. God sent me to teach people the right way; but I had to be taught before I could teach them, and you have to be taught, too, or you won't realize that there is a different life available to you.

SPEAK GOD'S LANGUAGE

Some people think they can tell what they call little white lies and still go to Heaven; but the Bible says that all liars, including the devil and his demons, will be cast into the lake of fire. **All liars, shall have their part in the lake which burneth with fire and brimstone: which is the second death** (Revelation 21:8). You may not lie, but do you whisper, backbite or pass on unnecessary information about other people? These things can do greater damage to you, your family and others than just lying. If Jesus would come when you're talking about someone, you'd be left.

Paul warned us about whisperers. **And even as they did not like to retain God in their knowledge, God gave them over to a reprobate mind, to do those things which are not convenient...whisperers, Backbiters, haters of God, despiteful, proud, boasters, inventors of evil things...Who knowing the judgment of God, that they which commit such things are worthy of death, not only do the same, but have pleasure in them that do them** (Romans 1:28–30,32).

When you have the love of God, it doesn't hurt anyone; it heals and comforts. If you want the love in the blood of Jesus to work for you, you have to be righteous. When you are, you will speak righteousness and holiness; but you have to want these things in order to have them.

God told me that His love is the divine picture of Jesus Christ, and you waste His shed blood when you're not perfect like Him and full of love. The Bible tells us that we're nothing without love. **Though I speak with the tongues of men and of angels, and have not charity [love], I am become as sounding brass, or a tinkling cymbal. And though I have the gift of prophecy, and understand all mysteries, and all knowledge; and though I have all faith, so that I could remove mountains, and have not charity [love], I am nothing** (I Corinthians 13:1,2). No matter what you may claim to be, you are nothing without divine love. Divine love is the only kind of love that's perfect; human love has imperfections.

When you keep talking about something over and over, you're holding on to it; you're not letting it go. People who have supposedly gotten saved and yet always talk about their sins aren't really saved. Those who dwell on all the things they used to do—drinking, taking drugs and running around with the wrong people—are not really ashamed of those things like they should be. When testifying, all they need to say is that they used to drink, smoke or take drugs; that's enough to let people know that they were once a sinner. No one should be proud of having been a sinner; instead, people should be proud that God delivered them. Tell others only enough about your past to enable them to realize that they too can be delivered. *People are either free or they're in bondage, saith the Lord.* You must emphasize to others that you're now free; and when you truly are free, your eyes will be on Jesus and not on the past.

GOD NEEDS YOU

God wants to be just as close to His children in this final hour as He was to Adam and Eve. He originally created man and woman so He could walk and talk with them, and He gave them a miniature mind like His own because He wanted them to be intelligent. What a beautiful time it must have been for the Father, the Son and the Holy Ghost as they walked with the man and woman they had made in the Garden where there was no sickness or despair. Adam and Eve had no tear ducts, and they never had to use the restroom; whatever they ate just evaporated. Our glorified bodies will operate the same way; we'll still be able to eat, but it will be purely for pleasure, and that will be wonderful.

CHAPTER 4

God's Waiting Room

*G*od is doing business on Earth today; and just as our earthly, medical doctors have a waiting room, God has one, too. The Bible says, **They that wait upon the LORD shall renew their strength; they shall mount up with wings as eagles; they shall run, and not be weary; and they shall walk, and not faint** (Isaiah 40:31). Even though you may have a specific appointment with your doctor, you might still have to wait; and there will be times when you have to wait on God, too. It's God's waiting room, but the Holy Spirit is in charge of it; and God sent Him to be our guide. He has to condition you first, and then He'll tell you when you're ready to go in because you may think you're ready before you really are. Until the Lord can reason with you 100 percent of the time, you're not ready. **Howbeit when he, the Spirit of truth, is come, he will guide you into all truth: for he shall not speak of himself; but whatsoever he shall hear, that shall he speak** (John 16:13).

You'll find Jesus in God's waiting room; and that makes it a divine room of love, patience, longsuffering and faith, one of goodness, mercy and grace. Some people think they're waiting upon the Lord when they're actually in the wrong waiting room. They're waiting for the wrong doctor in the wrong place, and they don't know it. They're looking forward to hearing the Holy Spirit say, "The Lord is ready to see you now"; but they'll never hear Him, and He can't direct them because they're in the wrong place.

The Holy Ghost gives you only the truth, so examine yourself spiritually. Are you living holy, glorifying God, being patient without grumbling and not wallowing in depression, oppression and despair? If you're all right, then you have to make sure you're waiting upon the Lord in the right place. Don't worry about wasting time because God has a purpose for everything He does. You may have to wait longer for some miracles than you do for others, but God will give you the grace you need as long as you're on obedient ground and ready for whatever God wants. I do all I can, and then I wait on Him; I don't contend with the Almighty.

APPROACH THE THRONE

God's waiting room has a big sign over it that reads, **Come now, and let us reason together, saith the LORD** (Isaiah 1:18). To reason with God means to listen to Him, realizing that your little mind is tiny compared to His great mastermind. God wants you to reason with Him, and you can by just presenting yourself before Him and saying, "Lord, I'm here to talk with you." He doesn't want you to be fanatical about it or use your imagination; He wants you to use your mind, face facts and accept *thus saith the Lord.*

Until you get rid of your theories and think like God thinks, you're not ready to go in before the throne and reason with the Lord. You first have to be justified and sanctified before you can go before it boldly. **Let us therefore come boldly unto the throne of grace, that we may obtain mercy, and find grace to help in time of need** (Hebrews 4:16). Through the blood, the throne of God has come down to us so that we can kneel before it any time of the day or night. We can go in before God with anything, even the daily requests we have regarding the building of His Kingdom.

God loves for us to hold onto lost souls who can be won, but He doesn't want us to waste our time and prayers on those who will never get right with Him. If you make every prayer count, God will let you know when you no longer need to pray for someone. I don't have time to waste my prayers; I need to pray for people throughout the world who have nobody else to pray for them.

You must use the blood for yourself and for others like never before in this last hour.

The blood is more valuable than all the silver, gold, diamonds and pearls on Earth. You're in the arena; and you're going to be tested and tried in unbelievable ways, especially in the mind. That's why the Lord moved on Paul to write to one of the churches, **Let this mind be in you, which was also in Christ Jesus** (Philippians 2:5). He told another church, **We have the mind of Christ** (I Corinthians 2:16).

Christ's mind was a healing mind, and His thoughts were healing thoughts. His mind was full of divine knowledge and divine wisdom, and it gave Him safety and protection. You have to take on the mind of Christ; but if you're bound with fear, you're just using your physical mind. You have to learn to gird your mind against the devil. **Wherefore gird up the loins of your mind, be sober, and hope to the end for the grace that is to be brought unto you at the revelation of Jesus Christ** (I Peter 1:13).

You're rich when you have the mind of Christ and are connected to Heaven, but the only way to be connected while here on Earth is through divine blood. The Bible says that His blood makes us nigh. **But now in Christ Jesus ye who sometimes were far off are made nigh by the blood of Christ** (Ephesians 2:13). Doesn't that excite you? I always pray through the blood, and I know God hears me every time.

A FAMILY OF PRAYER

My mama was a prayer warrior. I knew God answered her prayers, and that's why I had so much faith in her. She stood between me, God and Jesus so many times when I was a child. I didn't have to go to a teacher, preacher or anybody else for advice because I got all I needed at home. I'd unload my burdens on Mama, and she always took everything to the Lord no matter how busy she was. Sometimes, the Lord would give her the answer I needed right away; but if she didn't have the answer, she'd always say, "Honey, we'll pray about it." Because of Mama's faith, I saw many healings and miracles take place; and I had many answers to prayer. Mama had put so much of God into my mind that it all just dropped into my heart when I got saved.

Today, parents can instill that same faith into their children by having a family altar like we had in our home. A family altar is a place where the family gathers together at some time during the day and prays together. When that time came each day in our home, even as children, we knew we had to shut everything down. We didn't have to kneel down if we didn't want to; we could sit on a chair and bow our heads while those who were really serving God prayed. We were taught to honor God. If the Spirit of the Lord began to move and some wanted to linger in God's presence, we didn't have to stay. We could go to bed or quietly go back to whatever we had been doing, but we weren't allowed to disturb those who were praying.

We were used to hearing people pray out loud in our home. It wasn't unusual to wake up early in the morning and hear Mama praying. I try to get my congregation to pray out loud in their homes, too, because when loved ones hear others praying, it brings such a heavenly atmosphere to a home. Mom, Dad and my two older sisters would praise God and glorify the Lord; and sometimes the Holy Ghost would start speaking, first through one and then another. They wanted us to hear their prayers as they would call out our names before the Lord when we weren't living right, and I appreciated my family praying for me. I knew there was a hell, and I knew I didn't want to go there…and I knew God heard their prayers.

I wish every child could have a home like I had. God was real to me as I grew up. I didn't have to be saved to know that people were supposed to live holy, that there was a real God, a real Jesus and a real Holy Ghost and that the Holy Scriptures were the truth. I believed every word; and I knew that when I picked up the Bible, I was picking up the Lord Jesus. I was taught faith, and I knew that anyone who was sick in our home could be healed. Faith wasn't a stranger to me; but unfortunately, that kind of faith is a stranger to so many people today.

THINK GOD'S THOUGHTS

If you're not getting your prayers answered and the Holy Spirit is not ushering you in before the throne of God, it means you're not in the Lord's waiting room. You've missed it somewhere, and you must get back to that room or you'll never find the help you need. Instead, the devil will rob you, and you'll find yourself being disappointed in God. You can't expect Him to welcome you into His presence when you're disappointed in Him, and you can't be a disappointment to God and still be in the waiting room.

It's a great privilege to be in God's waiting room if you wait in divine truth with your whole heart. You can only get the results you need if you wait in total obedience, and that kind of obedience isn't moody. You allow the devil to take so much of your life when you're moody because moodiness is the spirit of the devil. Focus on being who you are just as Jesus was, and always remember you're a child of God.

I want to emphasize again that the waiting room is a place you have to be guided into so you can be taught by the Spirit Himself. You're to continually be coming into more and more knowledge of the truth, so you can't sit in the waiting room with an idle mind. You should think on these six things: **Finally, brethren, whatsoever things are true, whatsoever things are honest, whatsoever things are just, whatsoever things are pure, whatsoever things are lovely, whatsoever things are of good report; if there be any virtue, and if there be any praise, think on these things** (Philippians 4:8). Some of you never get to most of these thoughts in a day, so the devil is able to direct a lot of your thinking down the pathways of worry and fear. He scares you out of the blessings of God and out of His true and lovely thoughts.

We're not to think on things that are bad but rather on things that are of a good report. Good thoughts will keep our minds strong and fertile so they can receive more and more of the truths of God. **Blessed are they which do hunger and thirst after righteousness: for they shall be filled** (Matthew 5:6). Watch what you think about because your thoughts affect you more than you realize. If you're always thinking about sickness, then you're going to be sick. If you think about doubt, fear, frustration and despair, the devil will see to it that you have plenty of them.

It's easy to let the devil use your imagination because he's very sly about it; but if you use the blood, it will cleanse your thought life. **Casting down imaginations, and every high thing that exalteth itself against the knowledge of God, and bringing into captivity every thought to the obedience of Christ** (II Corinthians 10:5). The Word is truth, and it will cast down all imaginations if you'll let the Holy Spirit use it on you. So many believe for Him to use it on someone else, but they won't allow Him to use it on them.

The devil and self will give you the wrong thoughts; but be careful because the Bible says, **For as he** [a man] **thinketh in his heart, so is he** (Proverbs 23:7). Notice it says as he thinks in his heart, not in his mind. When the Holy Ghost seals a soul through the blood, the devil can't get in; so he tries to get in through the mind because it's not sealed. You have to know that you can still use the blood on your mind and allow the Holy Ghost to flow the love and deliverance of God through it.

And hope maketh not ashamed; because the love of God is shed abroad in our hearts by the Holy Ghost which is given unto us (Romans 5:5).

The Holy Spirit will use that love to cleanse our minds, and you can take as many flushes from Him as you need. There are days when I take many flushes because I can't keep all the things people unload on me in my head. I turn everything over to the Lord and let Him flush it out. Then He makes room for beautiful things.

FOLLOW ONLY TRUTH

Some of you are on dangerous ground because you've fallen away and are walking in the night, and God can't reason with you. You're full of disobedience and lust, and you're bathing in those things instead of bathing in the blood. Rather than drinking from the fountain of living water, you're drinking poison at the tree of death; and you're contaminated. But God can't stand contamination, and He'll cast you into hell if you don't get right with Him. You may be happy with your way of life now; but one split second after death, you'll know what a fool the devil has made out of you. The Lord warned us that this falling-away time would come. **Let no man deceive you by any means: for that day shall not come, except there come a falling away first, and that man of sin be revealed, the son of perdition** (II Thessalonians 2:3).

Lust is deadly like the devil himself; and although many people don't realize it, you can lust to satisfy the flesh with more than just sex. You can lust for houses, lands and possessions over and above what you really need. When the Lord brought the Israelites out of bondage, He loaded them down with the riches of Egypt. He made them wealthy with clothes, diamonds, pearls and all the best of Egypt; but later, they threw it all away when they made an idol god to worship, one they expected to take them back to Egypt. When they bowed down to that god, the Lord immediately destroyed about 3000 of them.

Those who have failed God think that false things are true and truth is false, but Jesus is all truth. **I am the way, the truth, and the**

life: no man cometh unto the Father, but by me (John 14:6). Jesus wants us to know that He is time and eternity; He is peace, joy, hope, happiness and our great I-Am. But if you don't know Jesus, you won't know the truth; and you'll be deceived in your own way of life. You'll fellowship with those who have failed or are disobedient, and you'll be blind to their sins.

You should never endorse that which is sinful and wrong, even if it's in your own family; but if you're not living close enough to God, you'll stand with them instead of standing for truth. Whenever you sympathize with those who are wrong, you'll become just like them. You'll be marked with the characteristics and traits of Jesus when you have them; but without them, you'll be marked by the devil. Present yourself before the Lord with a made-up mind and tell Him you're with Him to stay.

LEARN DIVINITY

You can't be in God's waiting room without His armor. You have to put on that armor before you go forth to meet each day just as you put on your clothes. Every morning,

God gives you a brand-new day to work for Him, to listen to Him and to learn more about Jesus. You have to take advantage of that opportunity and make sure you've done all you can do before you go into God's waiting room. Don't waste time asking God to give you things from His table that you can reach for yourself.

The more you learn about Jesus and accept all you learn in the same spirit in which the Holy Spirit teaches it, the more humble you will become. You have a teacher who teaches only divine truth; but unfortunately, divinity has not been taught like it should have been, and neither has the blood. I've spent thousands of hours with the Lord learning about the divine blood, and I'm still learning today.

Just as Daniel prophesied, knowledge has been greatly increased in this world. **But thou, O Daniel, shut up the words, and seal the book, even to the time of the end: many shall run to and fro, and knowledge shall be increased** (Daniel 12:4). But you must be knowledgeable in divinity; and the

Lord is making it possible for you to increase your spiritual knowledge every day, just as the world's knowledge is increasing. When I was born, there were no televisions, computers, CDs or even radios; but the world's techno-logical advancements are helping us take the Gospel to the whole world.

You can't be full of discouragement in God's waiting room. The devil has ground some of you down until you can't believe for the things that you need. He has focused your attention on those who are failing; but you must lift up your eyes unto Jesus, the author and fin-isher of your faith. **Looking unto Jesus the author and finisher of our faith; who for the joy that was set before him endured the cross, despising the shame, and is set down at the right hand of the throne of God** (Hebrews 12:2). Don't look at people; look for the blood-stained footprints of Jesus. He said, **Follow thou me** (John 21:22); and that says it all.

Jesus has made us the righteousness of God, which means we're His sons and daughters. **But as many as received him, to them gave**

he power to become the sons [or daughters] **of God, even to them that believe on his name** (John 1:12).

DON'T LISTEN TO THE DEVIL

Count your blessings, not your troubles. We don't have to worry about tomorrow because God is our high tower, and the Holy Spirit is our guide. He will give you a clear mind about the things of tomorrow. **Take therefore no thought for the morrow: for the morrow shall take thought for the things of itself. Sufficient unto the day is the evil thereof** (Matthew 6:34).

It's time for us to embrace only truth and to be honest with God, but first you have to be honest with yourself. Don't try to tell yourself that you can fail God, give over to the flesh and still go to Heaven because you'll never make it like that. *Thus saith the Lord, God is going to cut people off more and more in this final hour.* We're living in the hour of blasphemy that the Lord told me about years ago, and you can't let the devil or man influence you in the wrong way. The devil will try to worry you to death about what others are saying and doing, but you can't pay any attention to him. You have to focus your eyes on God.

When I got saved, I spent hours in God's presence; and I found the will of God because I wanted it. God taught me how to live in His very presence and how to listen to Him. He taught me how to totally depend on the Holy Spirit to guide me and how to get my answers from Heaven. You never have to beg God to do anything; just ask Him, and then close your case. Jesus didn't beg the Father for anything, not even in the Garden of Gethsemane, His most trying hour up to that time.

People who obey Satan and walk in darkness love the devil's power more than they do the power of God. God taught me this when I first received the gift of discerning of spirits. One time, when I was praying for a devil-possessed man, the demons swelled up in his neck; and people could see it. Oh, my God, he was a sight! It really scared people, but God let me know that the man loved the power of the devil.

When you obey the voice of the devil,

instead of looking for the footprints of Jesus, you're looking for ways to satisfy your own lust. You're covered with filth and dirt and don't want to be washed clean, and yet you claim to want to go to God's Heaven when you die. The Bible says, **The wicked shall be turned into hell, and all the nations that forget God** (Psalm 9:17).

All those who forget God will go to hell; and when you don't obey Him, you've forgotten Him. If children have godly parents and don't obey them, they've forgotten them. They're more interested in the things of the world than they are the righteousness and holiness of God. The world is full of filthy, rotten things; and hell is boiling over with all of that.

BELIEVE TO SEE

After Christ had been crucified, Thomas decided that he was through with Him. Even after Jesus' resurrection, Thomas doubted Him and boasted that he wouldn't believe Christ had been resurrected unless he could actually touch Him. **The other disciples therefore said unto him** [Thomas]**, We have seen the Lord. But he said unto them, Except I shall**

see in his hands the print of the nails, and put my finger into the print of the nails, and thrust my hand into his side, I will not believe (John 20:25). Thomas had forgotten everything the Lord had told him.

And after eight days again his disciples were within, and Thomas with them: then came Jesus, the doors being shut, and stood in the midst, and said, Peace be unto you (John 20:26). Jesus walked right through those closed doors and said to Thomas, **Reach hither thy finger, and behold my hands; and reach hither thy hand, and thrust it into my side: and be not faithless, but believing** (John 20:27). Suddenly, Thomas' doubt was all gone; and he said, **My Lord and my God** (John 20:28). Thomas had doubted and pouted for eight days, but you must never do those things. Even after Thomas was supposed to have received the Holy Ghost, the Bible never mentions anything about him doing any great works. God doesn't reward doubt.

All doubts and fears come from the devil; so without faith, you can't please God. **But without faith it is impossible to please him:**

for he that cometh to God must believe that he is, and that he is a rewarder of them that diligently seek him (Hebrews 11:6). God won't accept anything less than divine faith. He's God over all, and you must believe He will reward you for believing that all good things are possible through Him. Without divine faith, the promises of God won't work for you; they have to be connected with faith, and you'll find all the faith and divinity you need in the blood.

BE THANKFUL

If you're in the waiting room today and not using divine faith, you're not pleasing to God. You must enter into God's presence full of faith, thanksgiving and praise. **Let us come before his presence with thanksgiving, and make a joyful noise unto him with psalms** (Psalm 95:2).

Always remember the ten lepers who were cleansed and that nine never returned to say thank you. **And as he** [Jesus] **entered into a certain village, there met him ten men that were lepers, which stood afar off: And they lifted up their voices, and said,**

Jesus, Master, have mercy on us. And when he saw them, he said unto them, Go shew yourselves unto the priests. And it came to pass, that, as they went, they were cleansed. And one of them, when he saw that he was healed, turned back, and with a loud voice glorified God, And fell down on his face at his feet, giving him thanks: and he was a Samaritan. And Jesus answering said, Were there not ten cleansed? but where are the nine? There are not found that returned to give glory to God, save this stranger. And he said unto him, Arise, go thy way: thy faith hath made thee whole (Luke 17:12–19).

The Bible records nothing more about the nine, but the one who returned must have received his miracle of re-creation because Jesus said he was made whole. I'm sure his scars were all removed, and he had no signs of ever having had leprosy. The other nine probably carried their ugly scars for the rest of their lives, and some people may never have believed that they were even healed. They paid a price for not being thankful.

Sacrifice yourself before the Lord with a voice of thanksgiving, and never give up on God. When you're going through so much in His waiting room, always remember that you're helping others; and some may be your very own relatives. When friends and family think about you, they should also think about God because they should be able to see that you put all your trust in Him. The only way God may be able to bring some people to Calvary is by God using you, and don't ever forget that. God uses His people in many strange ways.

EGO IS DESTRUCTIVE

You must wait in the humility that took Jesus to the Cross. **And being found in fashion as a man, he humbled himself, and became obedient unto death, even the death of the cross** (Philippians 2:8). If you won't accept the Spirit's strict discipline and be obedient, the Lord said you could not be His child. **If ye endure chastening, God dealeth with you as with sons; for what son is he whom the father chasteneth not? But if ye be without chastisement, whereof all are partakers,**

then are ye bastards, and not sons (Hebrews 12:7,8).

God's children can have no ego, but there is so much of it today. God told me that ego comes from the devil, and the Lord can't use the spirit of the devil to do His work. Ego has destroyed many good people. Even many so-called Christians think they're more than what they really are in the Lord, but God is not fooled. The Bible says, **The Lord knoweth them that are his** (II Timothy 2:19). Those with ego may be deceiving themselves, but they're not deceiving God.

The Lord told me that He can't use people who lift themselves up in any way, and you need to stay away from people like that. Don't fellowship with those in darkness because people who are deceived will pass that deceit on to others. *They'll lead you to the tree of death, saith the Lord.* Are you deceived at all about yourself? The Lord said that deceit is a great hindrance. You may say, "I'm all right"; but you're not. You may say, "I don't gossip"; but you do. You may say, "I come to church all I can, I give all that I can, I fast every time the Lord moves on me to fast"; but you don't. You put everything off until tomorrow, but tomorrow never comes. Today is the day to get moving for God. **Behold, now is the accepted time; behold, now is the day of salvation** (II Corinthians 6:2).

AGREE WITH GOD

What are you working for? Are you busy building something for yourself or something for God? You're not going to be here much longer so why are you so concerned about yourself? To be all that God wants you to be, you have to slow down and wait on Him. You have to wait in divine love and in the divine faith that moves mountains, and you have to wait patiently.

Some of you allow yourselves to become irritable with friends, loved ones or those you work with. You may say things that hurt them, but the right kind of love will give you patience to discuss a problem in the light of the Holy Scriptures.

Can two walk together, except they be agreed (Amos 3:3)? The answer is no, and that's why there are so many divorces today.

Young people must keep themselves clean and marry someone who also lives clean. Couples must love each other with all of their hearts and decide to be patient, tender and kind to one another. Love doesn't hurt or destroy; real love heals.

How much have you studied the story of Gideon's fleece, and how much faith do you put in it? **And Gideon said unto God, If thou wilt save Israel by mine hand, as thou hast said, Behold, I will put a fleece of wool in the floor; and if the dew be on the fleece only, and it be dry upon all the earth beside, then shall I know that thou wilt save Israel by mine hand, as thou hast said. And it was so: for he rose up early on the morrow, and thrust the fleece together, and wringed the dew out of the fleece, a bowl full of water. And Gideon said unto God, Let not thine anger be hot against me, and I will speak but this once: let me prove, I pray thee, but this once with the fleece; let it now be dry only upon the fleece, and upon all the ground let there be dew. And God did so that night: for it was dry upon the fleece**

only, and there was dew on all the ground (Judges 6:36–40).

I've used fleeces down through the years to get answers from God; and when I do, that's always the final word. God answers my fleeces the way He chooses to, and then I go His way. There's no need to put out a fleece before God only to be disappointed and discouraged with the answer. You must say, "Thank you, God, for showing me the way and for making my paths plain. I love you, God, and I trust you with my whole heart."

Don't take up God's time and then not follow through on what He tells you to do. Have ears to hear Him or don't go into His waiting room. It's ridiculous to try to get to Him if you're not going to yield; you might as well just continue on your reckless way. You're just like a driver who is supposed to yield but doesn't and then nearly causes an accident. The driver isn't paying attention just as many people don't pay attention to God. Very few people really give God their whole hearts; their hearts are usually divided, and they only love God some of the time.

Many people start out running well with God, but then they stop. Would you want to take a ride with somebody who drives like that—someone who speeds up for a minute or two and then suddenly stops to worry and fret for a while? They may start moving again only to stop dead after just a short distance, and many people do that with God.

HAVE JOY AND PRAISE

You'll never bear fruit for the Lord by being inconsistent, and the Bride must bring forth much fruit. **Herein is my Father glorified, that ye bear much fruit; so shall ye be my disciples** (John 15:8). In this last hour, we have to abide in Jesus day and night just as the Early Church did; and they brought forth fruit in abundance. At one point, Peter had failed God and backslid completely; but when he got back to God and received the Holy Ghost, he won 3000 souls with just one sermon on the Day of Pentecost. **Then Peter said unto them, Repent, and be baptized every one of you in the name of Jesus Christ for the remission of sins, and ye shall receive the gift of the Holy Ghost. Then they that gladly**

received his word were baptized: and the same day there were added unto them about three thousand souls (Acts 2:38,41).

Joy is one of the fruits of the Spirit, and you must be full of joy and praise in God's waiting room because there's nothing in there to grumble about. You must wait in divine joy; and in this last hour, Heaven is bending down so low that you can reach up and get divine joy at any time. The Bible says, **Rejoice evermore** (I Thessalonians 5:16); and rejoicing will make you a good witness. When you serve doubt and despair, you're not a good witness; but when you serve happiness, it will come back to you and will also affect others. People notice those who are happy, and it will make them ready to hear about Jesus because they'll want to know where all your happiness comes from.

Happiness will bring peace, and you must be full of peace in God's waiting room. **And the peace of God, which passeth all understanding, shall keep your hearts and minds through Christ Jesus** (Philippians 4:7). Divine peace will enable you to put everything into God's care.

You must have the same forgiving spirit that Jesus had, and never forget that He forgave from the Cross. **Father, forgive them; for they know not what they do** (Luke 23:34). Stephen had that kind of forgiveness. **And they stoned Stephen, calling upon God, and saying, Lord Jesus, receive my spirit. And he kneeled down, and cried with a loud voice, Lord, lay not this sin to their charge. And when he had said this, he fell asleep** (Acts 7:59,60). Stephen was just like Jesus, even in death.

If you want to be like Jesus, you need to learn about yourself and know what makes you happy, sad, disappointed or depressed. I've made it my business to learn all about myself because I have to live with myself all the time. I have also made it my business to learn everything I can about the Holy Spirit and Jesus, and you must do that, too. You must know that when people receive the Holy Ghost, the first thing He does through them is glorify Jesus. The Holy Ghost was sent here to glorify Jesus, and Jesus was here to glorify the Father. What a marvelous plan!

SPEAK THE TRUTH

Are you a child of the King—a member of the Bride of Christ and the family of God? Are you contented to be God's child and to be with other true children of God? Do you like their holy conversation? Do you love to spend time in church, or do you sit in the pew thinking about all the other things you'd rather be doing? Believe it or not, some people even think evil thoughts during church; and God lets me know about it. When people speak, whatever is in them comes out in their voices. They create spiritual voiceprints, and they can't hide anything from God. However, if you have nothing but Jesus and divinity inside, you're glad for it to come out.

Jesus said, **For I have not spoken of myself; but the Father which sent me, he gave me a commandment, what I should say, and what I should speak** (John 12:49). Jesus only said what His Father gave Him to say; and people remarked, **Never man spake like this man** (John 7:46). That's the way it will be with the Bride; never before will people have heard anything like her. She will speak with an honest tongue of truth and tell the lovely story of the man called Jesus, our **KING OF KINGS, AND LORD OF LORDS** (Revelation 19:16).

I speak only the things of God. The Spirit takes me over, and the Lord uses my tongue as His very own; and I never forget the things that God tells me because I let them burn upon my heart. There are people who say that God told them something; but the next day, their story changes. God isn't like that. He said, **For I am the LORD: I will speak, and the word that I shall speak shall come to pass** (Ezekiel 12:25). You must hide such scriptures in your heart.

I love God's Word, and it will endure forever. **But the word of the Lord endureth forever. And this is the word which by the gospel is preached unto you** (I Peter 1:25). Yield to the Holy Spirit and study His Word. It will lift you up above the storms of life so that nothing can get you down. No human mind could have written the Word; it could only have come through the revelation of the Almighty. Then God sent Jesus, the revelation of all prophecies. *Through Him all prophecies have been and will be fulfilled, saith the Lord.* **And he** [Jesus] **said unto them** [His disciples]**, These are the words which I spake unto you, while I was yet with you, that all things must be fulfilled, which were written in the law of Moses, and in the prophets, and in the psalms, concerning me** (Luke 24:44).

What do you look like in the mirror of God's Word? **For if any be a hearer of the word, and not a doer, he is like unto a man beholding his natural face in a glass: For he beholdeth himself, and goeth his way, and straightway forgetteth what manner of man he was** (James 1:23,24). Some people look at themselves in a mirror so often that they no longer see any of their physical defects, but you can't get by that way with God. You have to know how you look in the light of God's holy Word because no one can get into Heaven unless he or she goes through the Word.

BE A SOUL WINNER

We're getting close to journey's end, and God is drawing those who are filled with the Holy Ghost. We can't just walk after Him; we have to run. The Bride is saying to her Groom, Jesus, **Draw me, we will run after thee** (Song of Solomon 1:4). We must run after His ways, His speech and His laughter. We must run after His peace, love, faith and hope. We must seek the great revelations of our Father in Heaven. You can't run after the world and the righteousness of Christ at the same time. You're either for Him or against Him; you either believe Him or you don't.

The Lord has marked many souls for each one of us to win, and we must not fail. When those souls come across our paths, we have to be ready. Soul winners must be alert, watchful and looking for Jesus to come. **He that winneth souls is wise** (Proverbs 11:30). **And they that be wise shall shine as the brightness of the firmament; and they that turn many to righteousness as the stars forever and ever** (Daniel 12:3). The Lord uses stars to represent souls, and I've seen the stars in my church auditorium coming down within reach; the people can just reach up and touch them. Loving hands of dedicated children of God become hands that use divinity, and they're full of divine faith and forgiveness.

CHAPTER 5

Healing for Soul and Body

How does divine healing come about? It comes through the grace of God, the works of God and the works of the Holy Spirit. It comes through divine blood, and no disease can stand before that blood. Why should we worry or fret when Jesus said, **Be not afraid, only believe** (Mark 5:36)?

Jesus spoke those words to Jairus right after he had been told that his daughter was dead, and then Jesus followed him to his house. When they arrived, the house was filled with mourners; but they were all hypocrites, and Jesus asked, **Why make ye this ado, and**

weep? the damsel is not dead, but sleepeth
(Mark 5:39). When Jesus said that, the people
suddenly stopped their mourning and started
to laugh and make fun; so Jesus threw them
all out of the house. Then He called the young
girl from the deep sleep of death just as if
she had been napping. **He took the damsel
by the hand, and said unto her, Talitha
cumi; which is, being interpreted, Damsel,
I say unto thee, arise. And straightway
the damsel arose, and walked; for she was
of the age of twelve years. And they were
astonished with a great astonishment** (Mark
5:41,42). That girl was only twelve years
old, but she became a great testimony to the
power of God.

A MIRACLE FAMILY

I was raised with miracles in my home.
When I was young, my dad had asthma; and
during his attacks, it would seem like he was
smothering to death. My big, strong daddy
would be rendered so weak and helpless that
it looked like every breath would be his last,
and his eyes would be wide with terror. One
night, Mama woke me in the wee hours of the

morning saying, "Honey, Daddy's dying!" I'm sure that Mama and my two sisters had already been up all night, and they had called for the pastor. After prayer, my dad was instantly delivered. The devil could never torture our family with that disease ever again because Daddy had his miracle.

My mother was a great believer, and I always knew that I'd get well when she'd lay her hands on me. As a youngster, I had a long illness that must have been cancer of the bone in my right leg; and it felt just like a wild animal was gnawing on that bone. The pain would be so unbearable that at times, I'd scream in agony; but Mama would always stay by me and pray all the night through if need be until the pain would stop. She'd always say, "Honey, God is going to heal you"; and she'd lay the Promise Book on me. She held on for months, and then the answer came just as God had promised.

When I was in my teens, my mama had pneumonia and was close to death. I was scared to death that we might lose her because you could hear her chest rattling all over the house as she gasped for breath. She couldn't speak, but she motioned for her Bible to be opened and laid on her chest. I was just a sinner at the time, but I had been nurtured in faith; so I believed in miracle power and the Word, and I knew God could heal Mama. We called for an evangelist to come and pray, and Mama was healed in an instant. Shortly after the preacher had gone, Mama was up, dressed and in the kitchen singing and praising God. You couldn't tell that she had ever been sick. That's what God can do!

That miracle always reminds me of Peter's mother-in-law who was sick of a fever; but after Jesus had prayed for her, she got right up and cooked for them. **And when Jesus was come into Peter's house, he saw his wife's mother laid, and sick of a fever. And he touched her hand, and the fever left her: and she arose, and ministered** [cooked or served] **unto them** (Matthew 8:14,15).

YOU CAN BE AN HEIR OF GOD

Unfortunately, most people have not had the background in faith that I had growing up; but that doesn't matter. When you come to the Lord, you can have divine faith. You can have all your doubts and fears erased because God's children are co-workers and joint-heirs with Jesus Christ. **The Spirit itself beareth witness with our spirit, that we are the children of God: And if children, then heirs; heirs of God, and joint-heirs with Christ** (Romans 8:16,17). That means you share equally in all that's His, and everything He has is good. That's what the divine blood and the grace of God are all about.

You're either going to use Christ's divine blood and claim what is yours or you're not. If you don't use it, you're wasting the most valuable thing in the whole world; and you can't get into Heaven without the blood. Heaven may be millions of miles away, but the blood makes it just one step away. That's what the blood has done!

Without that blood, there's no forgiveness for your sins. **And almost all things are by the law purged with blood; and without shedding of blood is no remission** (Hebrews 9:22). The blood has all power, but it can't work for you if you're in a lukewarm condition. **So then because thou art luke-warm, and neither cold nor hot, I will spue thee out of my mouth** (Revelation 3:16). The Lord means exactly that—He'll spew you out.

THE TRUTH ABOUT HOLY COMMUNION

The Lord offers you so much. Jesus came to set captives free, not to put them in bondage. Go back and study the Israelites. They were weak and sickly and had been almost destroyed through slavery; however, the blood made them whole when they took Holy Sacrament as God had instructed them to. When you take true Holy Communion, it's one of the greatest opportunities for you to receive any miracle you need if you're living holy before God. But woe be to you if you take communion when you're not living for God.

The church at Corinth was full of sin and death, and Paul wrote to them concerning some of their sins. Then he warned them that if they took Holy Communion without being worthy of it, they would drink damnation to their souls. **Whosoever shall eat this bread, and drink this cup of the Lord, unworthily,** shall be guilty of the body and blood of the Lord. But let a man examine himself, and so let him eat of that bread, and drink of that cup. For he that eateth and drinketh unworthily, eateth and drinketh damnation to himself, not discerning the Lord's body. For this cause many are weak and sickly among you, and many sleep (I Corinthians 11:27–30).

When you drink damnation to your soul, you can die at any moment; and it may not be God's time for you to go. In the Old Testament, Methuselah lived to be almost 1000 years old and no doubt had good health and strength all those years. But most people today don't even live to be 100, and some talk about getting old at forty. Old age isn't something to look forward to because it's not the divine plan of God.

DECEIT BRINGS DESTRUCTION

Some people think they can live degraded lives of the world and still receive healings from Heaven. What would you do if the Lord told you He was going to show your life on a big screen for all to see? You'd probably let out a scream like no one has ever heard before; but one day, all of your secrets will come out. Until then, if you don't get right, you'll continue to live in the deceit of Lucifer; and you won't even have sense enough to know it. When you believe a lie, you're dangling over hell; and you can drop into that awful place at any time.

I had a vision in which I was able to look down into the pits of hell, and I could see the smoke of the people's torment coming up toward me. God is going to wipe the memory of every person who has died without Him out of His mind forevermore. There will be no record of them in His book of life, and He'll never remember that they were ever born.

The Lord told me one time that He can hate as much as He can love. He said, **I also will laugh at your calamity; I will mock when your fear cometh** (Proverbs 1:26). A God full of hate who has turned deaf ears and blind eyes toward you will mean calamity. You will have no hope in this life or in the life to come, but there is hope in all things for true children of God; and that includes healing.

HEALING IS GOD'S WILL

You must know that it's absolutely the will of God for you to be healthy. In fact, physical healing is mentioned more in the four Gospels than any other doctrine or teaching—more than Heaven, hell and the judgments. Search the scriptures yourself, and they will bring you into the reality of the Savior who came and the divinity He brought. It is God's will to heal every child of God, so why do you hide behind a screen of, "I don't know whether God wants to heal me or not?" Step out from behind that fig-leaf religion and know the truth. **Behold, I am the LORD, the God of all flesh: is there anything too hard for me** (Jeremiah 32:27)?

God is a good God, and sickness only comes from the devil. Go back to Genesis, and you'll find that there were no sicknesses or tears in Eden until man sinned. When you talk about sickness, you're glorifying the devil. Don't tell people that you're in pain or that you can't get rid of some illness unless you're talking to a doctor or a preacher who believes in healing and miracles. It's worthless to tell others about your troubles. That won't bless them, and then they will have to overcome not only their own doubts and fears but yours, too.

If it's God's will to take one of His children home, sickness doesn't have to eat the life out of that person. I remember asking a woman one time, "Do you believe that God will heal you?" She answered, "I don't know because I've been sick for so many years." That was a ridiculous thought, and it didn't match the thought of God. God can heal you no matter how long you've had an affliction. If any of my thoughts don't match the thoughts of God, I get rid of them.

If people don't believe it's God's will to heal them, then why do they seek medical help from doctors? Those doctors would be working against the will of God, and that's ridiculous. A good doctor or nurse who recognizes God is a wonderful blessing, and I appreciated every medical person who helped me when I was in so much pain.

Now, I'm not suggesting that being sick means you have sinned or failed God because it does not. The devil has afflicted many godly people. If he can't get people to sin, he likes to torment and afflict them and make them suffer; but God wants His holy people to be well. **Beloved, I wish above all things that thou mayest prosper and be in health, even as thy soul prospereth** (III John 1:2). Our souls are to be free and prosper every day; and through the faith and grace of Heaven, our bodies should function the same way. No one has to have aches and pains or sicknesses and diseases. We're supposed to have the same health that Adam and Eve had before they fell.

Every good gift and every perfect gift is from above, and cometh down from the Father of lights [meaning from the throne of Glory]**, with whom is no variableness, neither shadow of turning** (James 1:17). God and His will never change. Sicknesses and diseases are not good and perfect gifts, so they can in no way come from the Father. God's good and perfect gifts belong to you, and Heaven has plenty of them—including the gift of good health. You can't enjoy the riches of God if your health is not good.

THE POWER OF THE WORD

For this purpose the Son of God was manifested, that he might destroy the works of the devil (I John 3:8). Jesus came to destroy all the works of the devil, and what are they?—sin and sicknesses. Jesus manifested Heaven's great love, power and divine blood so we could be saved, healed and delivered. The blood has life in it, and it's yours to use if you're a child of God. Without the blood, there could be no forgiveness for sins and no healings or miracles.

The miracle of all miracles is salvation; that's why Christ's ministry was a salvation and healing ministry. Souls were paramount, but the Lord also placed great emphasis on physical healing. The Bible tells us again and again that Jesus healed many people. **Great multitudes followed him** [Jesus]**, and he healed them all** (Matthew 12:15). Those multitudes were so amazed by His miracles that they would even follow Him into desert places.

In the Early Church, the Word multiplied. **The word of God grew and multiplied**

(Acts 12:24). The Word also went into operation and worked for people. **So mightily grew the word of God and prevailed** (Acts 19:20). Through faith, the disciples turned the power of the Word on; and they went everywhere preaching it. The Word prevailed over the powers of the devil, and sicknesses and devils were cast out.

The Bible tells us that at times, just the shadow of Peter coming over people brought deliverance. **And believers were the more added to the Lord, multitudes both of men and women. Insomuch that they brought forth the sick into the streets, and laid them on beds and couches, that at the least the shadow of Peter passing by might overshadow some of them. There came also a multitude out of the cities round about unto Jerusalem, bringing sick folks, and them which were vexed with unclean spirits: and they were healed every one** (Acts 5:14–16). Did Peter's shadow bring about the miracles?—No, the people just released their faith when it came over them. Only faith in God heals the sick, and divinity makes us well. Move in closer to the Lord where He not only will heal you but keep you healed. Never give up.

OLD TESTAMENT MIRACLES

Throughout the ages, God has healed His people; and here are a few examples of God's promises of healing put into action through Old Testament men of God. **So Abraham prayed unto God: and God healed Abimelech, and his wife, and his maidservants; and they bare children** (Genesis 20:17). That whole family was healed, including the slaves, when Abraham prayed. Abimelech received his miracle, and you can get yours, too. Don't make it hard. Jesus said, **Ask, and it shall be given you; seek, and ye shall find; knock, and it shall be opened unto you** (Matthew 7:7). Just ask, and you will receive. Seek means to desire it, and you will find it. Knock, and the door will open; but you have to have faith to step across the threshold.

The devil will try to scare you and stop you from holding on to receive your miracle. He'll say, "You had better not say you're healed because you might not be," or "See, you have a pain." *Some of you have gotten your miracle more times than one, saith the Lord; but you let the devil rob you of it.* You have had the miracle to take home with you, but you have to fight in order for divinity to work. If you're not going to fight and hold onto your miracle, then don't tell people that you got healed because they'll see that you really didn't; and that will hurt the work of the Lord. You have to believe it with all of your heart to receive just like you did when you got saved.

Remember the Shunammite woman who declared, "All is well!" even though her son had died. She had faith that God would raise him again, and she didn't take time for doubt. **Then she saddled an ass, and said to her servant, Drive, and go forward; slack not thy riding for me, except I bid thee. So she went and came unto the man of God to mount Carmel. And it came to pass, when the man of God saw her afar off, that he said to Gehazi his servant, Behold, yonder is that Shunammite: Run now, I pray thee, to meet her, and say unto her, Is it well with**

thee? is it well with thy husband? is it well
with the child? And she answered, It is well
(II Kings 4:24–26).

When Elisha sent his servant out to meet the
woman, she just brushed him aside saying,
"All is well"; and you can tell the devil and
your family members the same thing. When
all is well, then you can go on to do the will of
God and take your miracle; and that's exactly
what that woman did.

Elisha went to the woman's house to pray
for her son; and after stretching himself out
over the boy and seeking God, the boy's
life returned. **And the child sneezed seven
times, and the child opened his eyes. And
he** [Elisha] **called Gehazi, and said, Call this
Shunammite. So he called her. And when
she was come in unto him, he said, Take
up thy son. Then she went in, and fell at
his feet, and bowed herself to the ground,
and took up her son, and went out** (II Kings
4:35–37). The woman believed, fought for
the miracle and got results.

When Elijah was still on Earth, the Lord
had used him to raise the dead. **And he**

[Elijah] **stretched himself upon the child three times, and cried unto the LORD, and said, O LORD my God, I pray thee, let this child's soul come into him again. And the LORD heard the voice of Elijah; and the soul of the child came into him again, and he revived** (I Kings 17:21,22). These scriptures prove that the child was absolutely dead, but God raised him up.

CLOSE YOUR CASE

We've had the dead raised in this ministry, too. A man who had worked for this ministry for many years died, and the nurse on duty confirmed that he had no heartbeat or pulse for twenty minutes. My church members and I sought God the whole night through, and God brought him back to life. He lived several years after that, but he was never satisfied here on Earth because he had actually seen Heaven in those twenty minutes. He saw Angel sitting on one side of Jesus and an empty chair on the other side, but he couldn't get to them. He was very thirsty and looking for water, but he couldn't find the river of life. If he had, he never would have come back. Later, he did get to the river of life, and he didn't return; but he had been a great witness in the meantime. He gave his testimony in many churches, and people were overwhelmed by the reality of it.

The Lord wants to perform mighty miracles for all who will allow Him to, and He's drawing people; but some of you are not running after Him. You've received prayer many times; but you think that your miracle won't happen, and you haven't closed your case. When you receive prayer, you must close your case. When Jesus was on Earth, every time people closed their cases and kept them closed, they received a lasting miracle; but some people won't live up to their privilege in the Lord.

You have to expect miracles. I don't only believe in miracles, I depend on them. This ministry is a miracle work, but it never could have been without the gifts of the Spirit working in my life. Those gifts have made this ministry different, and we're working hard to build the Lord's Kingdom. Jesus said, **And this gospel of the kingdom shall be**

**preached in all the world for a witness unto
all nations; and then shall the end come**
(Matthew 24:14). We preach the Gospel;
and the Lord confirms it with signs, wonders,
miracles and healings in every service. God
wants to perform mighty miracles on you, too,
so that you will be a witness to others and be
able to help them to receive what they need.

Miracles catch on faster than any diseases
the devil has to offer, but the devil never stops
fighting. I've seen Jesus many times during
adverse circumstances; and in one of my crusade services, He appeared so big. There was
a bush near Him, and He turned and began
inspecting it. The next day, I asked the Lord
what He had been looking for; and He said,
"I was checking the fruit." We were gathering in the fruit by the thousands, and the Lord
was inspecting it.

I've learned so much about Jesus, and I've
learned that He loves for us to produce fruit
for Him; but we can't produce any fruit without first being connected to the vine. **I am the
vine, ye are the branches: He that abideth
in me, and I in him, the same bringeth forth**

much fruit: for without me ye can do nothing (John 15:5). Jesus also said, **Wherefore
by their fruits ye shall know them** (Matthew
7:20). This proves just how important it is to
have all of the fruits of the Spirit.

RECEIVE THE REAL HOLY GHOST

Jesus told the disciples not to start the
Church until they had received the Holy
Ghost. **And, behold, I send the promise of
my Father upon you: but tarry ye in the
city of Jerusalem, until ye be endued with
power from on high** (Luke 24:49). That is
exactly what the Lord's disciples did. **And
when the day of Pentecost was fully come,
they were all with one accord in one place.
And suddenly there came a sound from
heaven as of a rushing mighty wind, and
it filled all the house where they were sitting. And there appeared unto them cloven
tongues like as of fire, and it sat upon each
of them. And they were all filled with the
Holy Ghost, and began to speak with other
tongues, as the Spirit gave them utterance**
(Acts 2:1–4).

John the Baptist, the forerunner of Jesus,

prophesied that Jesus would baptize people in the Holy Ghost and with fire; and we have that same fire. **I indeed baptize you with water unto repentance: but he that cometh after me is mightier than I, whose shoes I am not worthy to bear: he shall baptize you with the Holy Ghost, and with fire** (Matthew 3:11).

Many Pentecostal churches today have lied to people about the Holy Ghost, and it has caused them to lose their power with God. Some have taught their people to speak and to sing in tongues at will, but that's not the real Holy Spirit. Speaking in tongues and prophesying at will come from ego and fanaticism, and they cause people to become devil possessed. *Many Pentecostals have gotten into the wrong spirit, and devils have taken many of them over, saith the Lord.* They've substituted their own tongue for the Holy Ghost tongue, but the Lord has warned me about this and said that it is not of Him.

Some people think they can speak in tongues any time they want to; but it just sounds like a rattle before God, and He hates it. People have to get the real Holy Ghost or they'll be left when the Rapture takes place. The Bible says we can only be changed according to the power that works within us. **But if the Spirit of him that raised up Jesus from the dead dwell in you, he that raised up Christ from the dead shall also quicken your mortal bodies by his Spirit that dwelleth in you** (Romans 8:11).

The real Holy Spirit is the Spirit of truth, and truth is the only thing He works through. **And I will pray the Father, and he shall give you another Comforter, that he may abide with you forever; Even the Spirit of truth; whom the world cannot receive, because it seeth him not, neither knoweth him: but ye know him; for he dwelleth with you, and shall be in you** (John 14:16,17).

THE BEAUTY OF GRACE

All of your needs are supplied by Jesus Christ—salvation, eternal life and healing for soul, mind and body. Jesus brought all the divinity we could ever use. The human nature failed, so only divinity can bring humanity into the great favor of God. You must realize that His grace is sufficient for you and that any weakness in your body can be made perfect through His grace. Paul learned that, and so must you. **And he said unto me, My grace is sufficient for thee: for my strength is made perfect in weakness. Most gladly therefore will I rather glory in my infirmities, that the power of Christ may rest upon me** (II Corinthians 12:9).

You must have reality in God, the Son and the Holy Ghost. If you don't learn divinity and how it works, you'll never receive what you need from Heaven. I had to learn how divinity works, and it's all laid out through Jesus Christ. He loads our tables daily with divine things, and He puts them within our reach. If you're walking in the divine will of God, you will want nothing but what He wants for you. You will have nothing but obedience and the knowledge of God's promises, and you'll be completely yielded to each and every promise.

God definitely wants healing for His children, and healing from Heaven should be the greatest thing in your life; but it all begins on the inside with your soul. When you're right with God, you can claim any of His promises as long as you meet their conditions. Every promise is conditional; and the Lord said that if you would repent with godly sorrow, you would be forgiven. **For godly sorrow worketh repentance to salvation not to be repented of: but the sorrow of the world worketh death** (II Corinthians 7:10). Godly sorrow means you're as sorry for your sins as God is sorry that you committed them, and that is the key to forgiveness.

Most of the inmates in prisons today are not sorry for the crimes they have committed; they're just sorry they got caught. Many people are the same way when it comes to their spiritual conditions—they're not truly sorry for their sins; they're just sorry they got caught. Some may say a little, worthless prayer to make themselves feel better, and others may go as far as trying to talk in tongues; but those things won't work. The real Holy Ghost can only use a holy tongue and nothing less.

Do you want reality in God? I received

that reality by studying divinity so I could recognize it. Then I fasted for great anointings that would enable me to receive it and use it. Now, I can use divinity just like you can shake hands with somebody; and you can use it, too, if you'll reach out for it and learn to hold onto it.

THE MINISTRY OF ANGELS

Angels are a part of divinity, and they're real to me. Are you conscious of them? The Lord started working with me in the ministry of angels by introducing me to one whom He calls His big angel. This big angel stands beside me in every miracle service, and I never pray for the sick without him being there because it takes the presence of the Lord to heal. The Lord told me that His big angel just turns from Him on the throne to talk to me; that's how close the connection is. That angel is so real to me that when He's touched me at different times, I've whirled around and started to say, "Excuse me." Then it dawns on me that it's the angel. He can touch me when I'm weary, and suddenly I have all kinds of strength.

Angel strength is mighty indeed. God sent

one angel to end a war by killing 185,000 enemy soldiers in one night. **And it came to pass that night, that the angel of the LORD went out, and smote in the camp of the Assyrians an hundred fourscore and five thousand: and when they arose early in the morning, behold, they were all dead corpses** (II Kings 19:35). When Jesus was agonizing in the Garden of Gethsemane, God sent an angel to strengthen Him. **There appeared an angel unto him** [Jesus] **from heaven, strengthening him** (Luke 22:43).

As I continued on in the ministry, the Lord came to me one day and said, "This ministry is going to be a ministry of angels." I pondered over that statement because I had no idea that I would ever work with angels, and it stirred my heart. Already, one angel had become so real to me that he could wake me at any hour to tell me things and to warn me about things coming up that God wanted me to know. He would direct me in where to go for my next crusade or give me anything else I needed from Heaven that would keep me in step with Jesus and on time with God. Angels carry the same expression of peace that Jesus has, and I love to look into their faces. Their eyes are so clear, and they bring such a beautiful presence from the throne of God.

Some time after the Lord had told me about all of this, I was conducting a service in North Carolina when suddenly the Lord let me know that angels were moving in to work with the people. He told me to tell those who had a deaf ear to hold up a finger and that the angels of the Lord would pass through the congregation and touch their fingers. I told the people what the Lord had said; and then I explained, "The angels will put the same power on your fingers that the Lord does on mine when I cast the deaf spirits out of people's ears." That was the beginning of my working with many angels, and the Lord was revealing to me exactly how it would work from that time forward. Since then, I've seen angels come into my services all dressed in white robes and fill the empty seats. That's why so many people are able to be healed.

The Bible tells us that angels will minister to true children of God. **Are they not all**

**ministering spirits, sent forth to minister
for them who shall be heirs of salvation**
(Hebrews 1:14)? I'm an heir of salvation,
and angels come to minister in my services.
They hold back the powers of darkness while
the Lord performs mighty miracles in abundance. Thousands of miracles can take place
in just a matter of moments in my overseas
crusades. In one nation, there were 12,000
people healed in just a few minutes of time;
the Lord numbered them Himself, and He's
the only one who can calculate such numbers.
He'll even tell me the initials and the afflictions of people who are about to be healed.

JESUS BROUGHT ABUNDANT LIFE

I live in such a close place with the Lord
that He can tell me whatever He wants me
to know, and you can live that same way; but
God will only talk to you if you're willing to
do all that He tells you to do. He won't keep
going after you if you're only going to give
Him fifty or seventy-five percent service. I
go all the way with God to do His whole will,
and you must do the same.

I weep for people in the world who have

never had an opportunity to know Christ. Untold millions are born into witchcraft, voodoo and all kinds of devil doctrines; but Jesus brought all the help they need. He brought abundant life above anything anyone could have ever imagined or experienced. **I am come that they might have life, and that they might have it more abundantly** (John 10:10).

Abundant life is a life of great happiness; it's a holy life like God Himself. Jesus gave up everything to bring us this abundant life. He came down to this sinful Earth unappreciated and without any favor. People hated Him and then killed Him, but they're burning in hell for it today.

Our supply comes only through Jesus Christ. Things which are intangible to most people become tangible to those who are serving the Lord in living reality. He makes divinity so real that you can see through the eyes of faith and hear what the Spirit is saying. The Lord has everything we need ready for us just like He had prepared the fish for the disciples and told them to **come and dine** (John 21:12).

YOU MUST BE RIGHTEOUS

Jesus has everything ready and waiting for you, but you have to prepare yourself for Him. You may think you have plenty of time to prepare, but you'll still be thinking those thoughts in your last minute before Satan's devils come to usher your soul into hell. God's divine gifts can't be bought with money, and nobody can buy their way into Heaven. Jesus and His divine blood provide the only passport; nothing else will be accepted.

Do you have the faith and courage to live for eternity, or do you walk in fear? You won't live in fear if you walk in God's love. Do you live in grace and are you satisfied with it? If you're not living holy, then divine grace isn't enough to satisfy you; but it would be if you'd let it be. You either live in grace or in disgrace; there's no in-between.

You must come into the reality of the faith of God, but do you know what that faith is? It's acting out exactly what God has said in the Holy Bible. You can find God's words if you have the right kind of heart, one that is cleansed and washed in the blood of Jesus Christ.

Do you abide in God's Word? His Bible says, **If ye abide in me, and my words abide in you, ye shall ask what ye will, and it shall be done unto you** (John 15:7). But how many qualify for this verse? Your soul has to be tuned in to the throne of the Father. Then you can ask what you will because you'll ask in the divine will of God, and the Holy Spirit will reveal that divine will to you daily.

You must clothe yourself in the righteousness of God. The Bible says, **For God hath not called us unto uncleanness, but unto holiness** (I Thessalonians 4:7). Jesus had nothing else to call us to but holiness; yet so many people hate the word holiness, and they hate godly people. You must decide what moves you—God's choices or your choices.

DON'T BE FOUND WANTING

Not being satisfied is what causes people to grumble and complain and to be full of doubt and fear, and that's exactly what happened to the Israelites. Although they left Egypt physically, they never left it spiritually. They were just like some people today who leave the world enough to go to church but not enough to live holy and keep themselves from satisfying the lust of the flesh.

The Israelites saw so much of the grace and the glory of God, but they still wouldn't follow Him. They witnessed all of the miracles God used to bring them out of Egypt, and they saw the greatest miracle of all when God separated the waters of the Red Sea just for them. **With the blast of thy nostrils the waters were gathered together, the floods stood upright as an heap, and the depths were congealed in the heart of the sea** (Exodus 15:8).

Although many people today deny that the Israelites actually crossed on dry land, archaeologists have found chariot wheels and other things from that great event. God has kept them there all of these years and is allowing them to be brought out in this final hour. I know the waters separated because God said they did, and it wasn't just a spiritual crossing.

Do you really believe all that God says? Are you walking all the way with the Lord or just part of the way? Are you following all of His paths or are you divided? You must weigh as much in divinity as Jesus did when He walked among men. Some people are more concerned about their physical weight than they are about their spiritual weight, but they'll be weighed in God's balances and found wanting just as Belshazzar was. **Thou art weighed in the balances, and art found wanting** (Daniel 5:27).

Belshazzar thought he was an important man and that he could do anything he wanted to and get by with it, but he was just a weasel in the eyes of God. He knew about his father, Nebuchadnezzar, and how God had punished him. The Lord had taken out his human heart and replaced it with the heart of an animal; and for seven years, he grazed in the fields and ate grass like an ox. When the seven years were over, the Lord restored his human heart to him; and he glorified God as the only true and living God. **And at the end of the days I Nebuchadnezzar lifted up mine eyes unto heaven, and mine understanding returned unto me, and I blessed the most High, and I praised and honoured him that liveth forever, whose dominion is an everlasting**

dominion, and his kingdom is from generation to generation (Daniel 4:34).

Belshazzar knew all of this; but still God's
accusation was, **The God in whose hand thy
breath is, and whose are all thy ways, hast
thou not glorified** (Daniel 5:23). That same
night, Belshazzar was slain; and when you
wallow around in sin without glorifying God,
you're subject to be cut off at any time, too.
The next hour could be your last one, and you
may never have another chance to repent.

LIFT UP JESUS

The Israelites' constant grumbling and
complaining angered God so much that at
one time He sent fiery serpents after them.
**And the LORD sent fiery serpents among
the people, and they bit the people; and
much people of Israel died.** When you sin
against God, you're in trouble. **Therefore
the people came to Moses, and said, We
have sinned, for we have spoken against
the LORD, and against thee; pray unto
the LORD, that he take away the serpents
from us. And Moses prayed for the people.
And the LORD said unto Moses, Make thee**

a fiery serpent, and set it upon a pole: and it shall come to pass, that every one that is bitten, when he looketh upon it, shall live (Numbers 21:6–8).

The word "looketh" means to continue to look, so you can't just look at God once; you have to continue to look. **But whoso looketh into the perfect law of liberty, and continueth therein, he being not a forgetful hearer, but a doer of the work, this man shall be blessed in his deed** (James 1:25).

The serpent of brass was a type and a shadow of the sacrifice Jesus made as He hung on that cruel Cross on Golgotha. **And as Moses lifted up the serpent in the wilderness, even so must the Son of man be lifted up** (John 3:14). We must always be lifting Jesus up.

King Jeroboam had sinned against God, and God crippled his hand; but God also used that to show him His greatness. **And the king answered and said unto the man of God, Entreat now the face of the LORD thy God, and pray for me, that my hand may be restored me again. And the man of God besought the LORD, and the king's hand**

was restored him again, and became as it was before (I Kings 13:6). God is ready to show people His greatness, but they have to know how to use His spiritual senses if they want to see it and hear it. You can't see or hear divine things with your own physical senses.

RECOGNIZE GOD MOVING

Jesus told people that they were spiritually blind and deaf because they wanted to be. **And in them is fulfilled the prophecy of Esaias, which saith, By hearing ye shall hear, and shall not understand; and seeing ye shall see, and shall not perceive: For this people's heart is waxed gross, and their ears are dull of hearing, and their eyes they have closed; lest at any time they should see with their eyes and hear with their ears, and should understand with their heart, and should be converted, and I should heal them** (Matthew 13:14,15).

What kind of eyes and ears do you have? Can the Holy Spirit verify that you're hearing all that He is saying? In times of trouble, you can be deaf to the things the Holy Spirit is trying to tell you because you're making so much noise with your own cries of doubt and pity.

The Word, Jesus, has a loud voice; but you have to have holy ears to hear what the Spirit is saying through it. The Spirit always gives you the Word and the promises of God and nothing less. Many times, He'll just bring one phrase to your mind. When convicting sinners, the Holy Spirit usually uses just one little phrase that He turns over and over in a person's mind until the Adamic nature begins to move out.

NOTHING BETWEEN YOU AND YOUR GOD

You have to treasure God above everybody and everything. I loved Angel with all of my heart, but I never let her get between me and God. We were both marked in our mothers' wombs for each other, and we fit so well together; we never argued or fought. Many couples have a rough time adjusting to each other after marriage, but Angel and I never did. We both had been given a foundation of holiness and righteousness, and we were vessels that He had marked to carry the Gospel to the world.

Angel had a personality that was so much like Jesus. She never gossiped, and she could turn away wrath in a moment with her kind words. She had so much love and lived so close to God that she was beautiful inside and out. She had promised me that she'd go anywhere God wanted me to go and that she'd always hold my hands up…and she never failed that promise. She loved to work with young people; and she'd talk to them about what it meant to pray, to serve God and to live holy. She taught them that they must remain virgins until their wedding day, and she knew what it meant to be a holy, uncontaminated bride.

I thought that Angel would always be with me, but calamity struck when the Lord suddenly took her home. Through that unbelievable valley of her death, I wanted to die for the first time in my life; but I never resented God for taking Angel home. I've always thanked Him that she's in Heaven where nobody can hurt her or make her cry; however, I was in a million pieces, and I had momentarily lost sight of the vision of bringing in the harvest for the Lord. I knew that only God could put me back together again, and I knew I had to live for my congregation.

Angel had given me so much love, but suddenly it was gone. I'd cry, "Lord, love me! I can't live without love"; and He would come down to me. He was so patient; and hundreds of times He would speak and say, "I am the Lord that walketh with thee." He knew what I was going through, and He was always there.

One day, I was down on the floor in Angel's office crying my heart out; and I don't know whether it was Jesus or an angel, but it felt just like a human arm had wrapped around me. The Lord gave me such help that day, and no one will ever know what that meant to me. Oh, I cried again after that, and I still hurt; but it was never as bad.

The Lord put me back together with great love and care as only He could have done, and He made me stronger than ever. I didn't know that I could ever receive so much life while here on Earth or that I could ever be happy again, but I'm truly one of the happiest people in the world. The Lord helped me to climb out of that deep, deep valley to get to the high mountain of God where I could give more of my life than ever to help others. When the time comes that I can't win any more souls, I'll be finished with this life on Earth because I have to have souls. Only God knows how many times that I've told Him that. I live for God, and I live to win souls!

CHAPTER 6

Psalms of Faith and Encouragement

We can have a wonderful life in Jesus, and the book of Ruth gives us a beautiful example of that. Because of a famine in Judah, Naomi, her husband and her two sons had gone to live in Moab; and while they were there, her sons married Moabite women. Later, both of Naomi's sons and her husband died, and she decided to return to her country alone.

Naomi's two daughters-in-law started on the journey with her, but one of them loved the idol gods of the Moabite people and decided to turn back. She hadn't really given her heart to Jehovah God, so she didn't want to go to the land of His people. Ruth, on the other hand, did want God; and she said, **Entreat me not to leave thee, or to return from following after thee: for whither thou goest, I will go; and where thou lodgest, I will lodge: thy people shall be my people, and thy God my God: Where thou diest, will I die, and there will I be buried: the LORD do so to me, and more also, if aught but death part thee and me** (Ruth 1:16,17).

Ruth kept that promise, and the Lord blessed her abundantly. She eventually met a godly man, Boaz, and she became the mother of many. She was told, **The LORD recompense thy work, and a full reward be given thee of the LORD God of Israel, under whose wings thou art come to trust** (Ruth 2:12). That's a beautiful thought!

The book of Ruth presents a vivid type and shadow of the spiritual Bride and Groom. Ruth was a type of the Gentile Bride, and Boaz was a type of our Groom, Jesus. According to the Law, Ruth, a Gentile, couldn't have become Boaz' bride; but through grace she did become his bride. Her story is a wonderful one of how the Law worked and how grace stepped in and took over. Ruth came forth with great favor, and at one point **Boaz commanded his young men, saying, Let her glean even among the sheaves, and reproach her not: And let fall also some of the handfuls of purpose for her, and leave them, that she may glean them, and rebuke her not** (Ruth 2:15,16). "Drop handfuls on purpose for her." That's a great message, and that's what the Lord is doing for the Bride today.

REST IN THE LORD

The Lord wants to give us handfuls on purpose. Think about how big just one of the Lord's divine hands must be and all it must be able to hold. God can hold the whole world in just one hand, so don't you think His hands are big enough to heal your whole body? If you're saved, you know He healed your whole soul, so why not your body? I never doubt anything God tells me no matter how impossible it may seem because I know that all things are possible with the Lord.

When God makes a promise, He keeps it; so I'm determined to keep any promise I make to the Lord, too.

Ruth found rest in the care of Boaz, and the Bride is to find rest under the wings of Jesus. You have no reason to worry about anything; and that's why the Bible says, **Be careful for nothing; but in every thing by prayer and supplication with thanksgiving let your requests be made known unto God** (Philippians 4:6). Some of you let worry ruin your sleep and wreck your nervous system. You're restless; you have nightmares, and everything disturbs you. But I've told you that if you use the blood and go to sleep in the blood, it will take care of all of your nightmares.

If you haven't come to rest under the wings of the Almighty, there's a resting place waiting there for you. Don't deceive yourself and pretend you're using the peace that's available under His wings if you're not. I have peace that comes only from the Lord, not from people. Divine peace is the only kind that is real and lasting.

PSALM 91

There are three very special psalms that can help you, and it would do you good to memorize them. I make sure that I hide plenty of the Word in my heart so that if someone were to take my Bible away from me, I'd still be all right. I would know my way through the Lord because I make it my business to know God and His promises and to know how to walk and talk with Him.

Psalm 91 is the first one I want to bring before you, and it tells of the rest and protection you will find in the Lord. **He that dwelleth in the secret place of the most High shall abide under the shadow of the Almighty** (Psalm 91:1). People who do not walk close to God and are not born new will never find that secret place. That secret place is as close to the Lord as a shadow is to a person, and you have to stay very close to a person to be under their shadow.

I will say of the LORD, He is my refuge and my fortress: my God; in him will I trust (Psalm 91:2). Notice the ownership in this verse—*my* refuge, *my* fortress and *my*

God. I weigh each word of God.

God is our protector and our fortress, so we have nothing to fear because the devil can't break through His fortress. The devil couldn't break through to Job, and he admitted it. **Doth Job fear God for nought? Hast not thou made an hedge about him, and about his house, and about all that he hath on every side? thou hast blessed the work of his hands, and his substance is increased in the land. But put forth thine hand now, and touch all that he hath, and he will curse thee to thy face** (Job 1:9–11).

The devil was sure that Job only served God because of what He had given him, but God knew that was a lie because Job's past record had not showed that. There was a time when Job was a poor man and didn't have anything; but he had loved God, and God had blessed him and brought him into all that he had.

GOD, THE DELIVERER

Surely he shall deliver thee from the snare of the fowler, and from the noisome pestilence (Psalm 91:3). This verse promises you that God will deliver you and keep you free from sicknesses and diseases, but some of you always expect to be sick.

He shall cover thee with his feathers, and under his wings shalt thou trust: his truth shall be thy shield and buckler (Psalm 91:4). Do you know what the Lord's feathers are? They're gentleness and goodness, two of the fruits of the Spirit. Have you ever seen a feather that wasn't gentle? I love to put my head on the Lord's feathers and go to sleep. The feathers of love, grace and faith that He offers will give you rest and calm your body. They'll let you know that all is well.

This verse also speaks of trust; and if you're not trusting in the Lord for everything, then you need to get under the wings of the Almighty. There you will find protection from all the powers of the devil, and he has never been able to defeat God's wings of protection for His people.

BE NOT AFRAID

Thou shalt not be afraid for the terror by night; nor for the arrow that flieth by day (Psalm 91:5). The Lord tells you that you're not to be afraid, so why are you?—because you're carrying something from the devil, the very one God wants you to hate. The Bible tells us how to get rid of fear: **There is no fear in love; but perfect love casteth out fear: because fear hath torment. He that feareth is not made perfect in love** (I John 4:18). When you get saved, it's through the perfect sacrifice of perfect love; so when you're truly free, you won't be possessed with fear. But if you fail to use God's love, you'll never get rid of fear. No one can scare it out of you, and you can't pray it away when you won't use love. God can anoint you with love and grace; but when you go from grace to fear and from faith to doubt, the anointing is of no use.

This is not a time to be afraid; but the Lord said that in the last days, many would be. **Men's hearts failing them for fear, and for looking after those things which are coming on the earth: for the powers of heaven shall be shaken** (Luke 21:26). More people are having heart trouble today than ever before; but when I was young, you seldom heard of anyone suffering with or dying from a heart attack. Some people get so stressed and depressed that they think they're having heart trouble when they're actually just feeling pressure. When children of God feel that way, they just need to crawl under the Lord's loving feathers.

Nor for the pestilence [the sickness] **that walketh in darkness** (Psalm 91:6). The sicknesses that afflict you come from the devil, not from Heaven. Divine light heals and brings life, but darkness is death. **Nor for the destruction that wasteth at noonday** (Psalm 91:6). When you're afraid, you waste beautiful, sunny days and the comfort and peace available to you through God.

DIVINE PROTECTION

A thousand shall fall at thy side, and ten thousand at thy right hand; but it shall not come nigh thee (Psalm 91:7). Not only will God fight for you, but He will also send angels to fight for those who are true children of God. We have already studied the ministry of angels in Hebrews 1:14, but some of you don't weigh every Word of the Lord. If you don't do that, you won't have the faith to use them.

Only with thine eyes shalt thou behold and see the reward of the wicked. Because thou hast made the LORD, which is my refuge, even the most High, thy habitation (Psalm 91:8,9). You'll see your enemies being defeated, but you won't be defeated. If you think you will be, it's just because the devil's fooling you and trying to make you think that you're not saved when you really are born new and living holy. No one can live holy without Heaven's salvation, and you're a hypocrite if you pretend to be holy when you know very well that you're not. If you're taking part in any unholy acts, you're unclean; and hell will be your destiny when you take your last breath. Every person on Earth today is either one breath away from hell or one breath away from Heaven. It's dangerous to be without God, and there's not enough money in the world to convince me to be without Him for one moment.

There shall no evil befall thee, neither shall any plague come nigh thy dwelling (Psalm 91:10). Evil will come, but it can't conquer you unless you yield to it. You must stand up tall and be holy, pure and clean. This verse also promises you that you can be well all the time if you'll use the blood. The only way you should suffer is like Jesus suffered— through persecutions. God doesn't will for us to suffer in any other way. **Blessed are they which are persecuted for righteousness' sake: for theirs is the kingdom of heaven** (Matthew 5:10).

Some people are persecuted because they're busybodies with long tongues, and all they want to talk about are their own problems and persecutions. The Lord said that such people don't belong to Him. **If any man among you seem to be religious, and bridleth not his tongue, but deceiveth his own heart, this man's religion is vain** (James 1:26). If you cause your own suffering, God can't help you.

For he shall give his angels charge over thee, to keep thee in all thy ways. They shall bear thee up in their hands, lest thou dash thy foot against a stone (Psalm 91:11,12). Once again, we are promised angel help, and angels ministered to me so much when the

Lord took my dear Angel home to be with Him.

POWER FROM ON HIGH

Thou shalt tread upon the lion and adder: the young lion and the dragon shalt thou trample under feet (Psalm 91:13). That's a powerful promise! God's promises are real, and He has told me that you will find all the powers of Heaven in each one. That's how strong just one promise from God is.

Because he hath set his love upon me, therefore will I deliver him: I will set him on high, because he hath known my name (Psalm 91:14). When you know the Lord's name, you can say, "My Father which art in Heaven"; and He really is your Father through divine blood. You're in the family of God just as much as His Son, Jesus, is; and He loves you with the same kind of love.

He shall call upon me, and I will answer him: I will be with him in trouble; I will deliver him, and honour him (Psalm 91:15). Any time a child of God calls, the Lord will answer because He's always on duty for us. God didn't say that He would be with us just

in the good times, but some people only recognize God being with them when everything
is rosy and the sun is shining. Some rain must
fall in each life here on Earth, and that's why
we have Jesus to take care of it all. He'll not
only deliver us, but He'll honor and bless us
and give us armfuls on purpose. **With long
life will I satisfy him, and shew him my
salvation** (Psalm 91:16).

PSALM 103

**Bless the LORD, O my soul: and all that
is within me, bless his holy name** (Psalm
103:1). This refers to a life that's given
wholly to the Lord—every nerve, every joint
and every bone. The whole body and soul are
to bless His holy name. The Lord said, **Be ye
holy; for I am holy** (I Peter 1:16).

**Bless the LORD, O my soul, and forget
not all his benefits** (Psalm 103:2). We must
remember every one of God's benefits. The
more time you spend remembering His benefits for you, the less time you'll have to worry
about your troubles.

**Who forgiveth all thine iniquities; who
healeth all thy diseases** (Psalm 103:3). God

forgives all of your sins, but He doesn't stop there; He also heals all of your diseases. It's wonderful to be free and to have good health.

Think about all of the people who are suffering in hospitals today and need Jesus. I thank God for all of our wonderful hospitals and clinics; they are houses of mercy, love and compassion that serve suffering humanity. However, we have to remember that medical science is limited, and that's why we must know that God is always ready to do for us what no other power can do. That's divine faith! We carry God's anointing in our bodies; it's God's healing from Heaven and the cure for everything. Decide that diseases can't live in you and that you'll use the blood for yourself and for others. Claim it and hold onto it.

Who redeemeth thy life from destruction (Psalm 103:4). Jesus came to redeem us from the destruction of all ungodliness and everything that is unclean, but think of the billions of people who are screaming in hell today because they wouldn't listen. Things will never change for them; eternity in hell will never end!

Who crowneth thee with lovingkindness and tender mercies (Psalm 103:4). Think about the patience, the tenderness and the care God has for us. Many people think there's not a more tender touch than that of a mother, and in the human that's true; but God's touch is far greater.

GOD WILL RENEW YOUR YOUTH

Who satisfieth thy mouth with good things; so that thy youth is renewed like the eagle's (Psalm 103:5). Not only can Jesus heal you, but He can add many years to your life. Remember the story of King Hezekiah. Isaiah, a great prophet of God, told him to set his house in order because he was going to die. But Hezekiah was a good king, and he already had his house in order; so he wept before the Lord saying, **I beseech thee, O LORD, remember now how I have walked before thee in truth and with a perfect heart, and have done that which is good in thy sight** (II Kings 20:3).

The Lord knew Hezekiah spoke the truth,

so the Lord gave Isaiah a second message for the king. **Turn again, and tell Hezekiah the captain of my people, Thus saith the LORD, the God of David thy father, I have heard thy prayer, I have seen thy tears: behold, I will heal thee…And I will add unto thy days fifteen years** (II Kings 20:5,6). God gave Hezekiah fifteen more years.

God did the same thing for my daddy. According to his doctors, he had suffered a very severe heart attack; but when a member of my family and I went to the hospital and prayed for him, the Lord re-created his heart. That night, he woke up at about 4 a.m. and decided to take a walk. It scared the nurse half to death because she had been given strict instructions to keep him in bed; but when the doctors examined him, they were totally amazed because they couldn't find one thing wrong with his heart.

God said in this psalm that He would renew our youth, but I can't get some of you to believe that. You're too busy complaining about your arthritis, but I wouldn't claim it. I'd say, "I'm getting a miracle because

I'm using the blood, and it will take away this arthritis." Don't claim diseases such as arthritis, heart trouble or cancer because when you do, you're reaching out to possess things that come from the devil. If you have cancer, realize that it comes from the devil and know that cancer melts before the power of God.

YIELD TO JUSTIFICATION

The LORD executeth righteousness and judgment for all that are oppressed (Psalm 103:6). God will take care of all of our enemies. **Vengeance is mine; I will repay, saith the Lord** (Romans 12:19). When I'm being persecuted, the Lord has taught me to say nothing; and He always takes care of the situation. Some of you try to fight your own battles, and that's why you don't come out on top. Fighting your own battles will only make you sick; so learn to lean on the Lord, to trust Him and to believe Him all the time. Learn to live by faith and to be justified through His precious blood.

The words of a beautiful song say, "I will never walk alone; He holds my hand." That song means so much to me, and the words followed me day and night when I was going through one of my deepest valleys. Because I had answered the call of God, I had to leave preachers behind whom I had worked with for years. I also had to leave the denomination that I had been raised in, and I had never imagined that I would have to do such a thing; but God was calling me away because many of the preachers were rejecting His power. True miracles only come through God's power.

You can't let anything hinder you or bother you. Some of you may have to pay a great price to walk away from the world, from your dead church or from your unsaved family and friends; but you must do it if you want to walk with King Jesus.

When Jesus was here, He prayed for our sanctification. **Sanctify them through thy truth: thy word is truth. As thou hast sent me into the world, even so have I also sent them into the world. And for their sakes I sanctify myself, that they also might be sanctified through the truth** (John 17:17–19). Jesus is truth, and we're sanctified through His blood.

In the Old Testament, God made His ways known unto Moses; and He made His acts known unto the Children of Israel. He made Himself real through divine miracles, the pillar of fire and the blood of animals. Because Jesus had not yet come, that blood represented divine blood; and it stayed the hand of death for the Israelites in Egypt. God performed many miracles that were a curse to the Egyptians, yet the Israelites still doubted God. Moses and God had a hard time getting the Israelites out of Egypt; and even after they had come out, the people wouldn't remain believers. Still today, many people are only temporary believers, and that's why it's so hard for them to hold on to what they receive.

GOD'S GREAT MERCY

The LORD is merciful and gracious, slow to anger, and plenteous in mercy (Psalm 103:8). The Lord is merciful and has everything you need, but the devil wants to make you forget that so you won't use God's mercy. If you don't use the things God has made available to you, it won't matter how great your need is for something because God won't be able to move for you. If you don't use your money, you can't buy anything; and if you refuse to eat, you'll eventually starve to death, even though you had plenty of food available to you.

He will not always chide: neither will he keep his anger forever (Psalm 103:9). God does get angry, and sometimes He gets so angry toward a person that He doesn't get over it; it all depends on how people react to the anger of God.

He hath not dealt with us after our sins; nor rewarded us according to our iniquities (Psalm 103:10). If God rewarded us for our iniquities, we'd all be in hell. **But God commendeth his love toward us, in that, while we were yet sinners, Christ died for us** (Romans 5:8). We have to realize just how merciful God was to us to let us live when we were sinners. Some of you were raised without knowing the first thing about God, His salvation or the fact that you could be born new.

For as the heaven is high above the earth, so great is his mercy toward them that fear

him (Psalm 103:11). To fear God means to honor Him, not to be afraid of Him. No good, loving mother or dad wants their children to be afraid of them; they just want to be honored and respected. God is our heavenly Father, and He doesn't want His sons and daughters to be afraid of Him either.

As far as the east is from the west, so far hath he removed our transgressions from us. Like as a father pitieth his children, so the LORD pitieth them that fear [or honor] **him** (Psalm 103:12,13). Jesus taught us to give honor where honor is due; but if honor is not due, He doesn't require us to give it.

WE ARE NOTHING WITHOUT GOD

For he knoweth our frame; he remembereth that we are dust (Psalm 103:14). God knows all about our physical bodies, and He knows that we're only made of dust. That's why He has furnished us all the strength of Heaven. Adam and Eve had no troubles in Eden until they sinned. Then they became weak; and because of their sin, we were all born weak.

No one is born in perfection outside of

Eden. **As for man, his days are as grass: as a flower of the field, so he flourisheth** (Psalm 103:15). No one is promised tomorrow no matter how important they may think they are. The Lord said, **Boast not thyself of tomorrow; for thou knowest not what a day may bring forth** (Proverbs 27:1). How many people were alive yesterday but are dead today? How many of them thought they would die, and how many were ready to go?

For the wind passeth over it, and it is gone; and the place thereof shall know it no more (Psalm 103:16). We see many beautiful flowers, but they all eventually decay. Thank God, we're going to a city where the roses never fade.

But the mercy of the LORD is from everlasting to everlasting upon them that fear him, and his righteousness unto children's children; To such as keep his covenant, and to those that remember his commandments to do them (Psalm 103:17,18). You must be conscious of God's Word every day and always keep the Lord before you if you want the Lord to keep you before Him. Never let

Him out of your sight, and never allow anything to crowd in and blind you. Do you see
the Lord all the time or do you lose sight of
Him at times? If you do, you're headed for
severe trouble; and you may never come out
of it.

  **The LORD hath prepared his throne in
the heavens; and his kingdom ruleth over
all** (Psalm 103:19). God has all power, and
that power belongs to us. When Jesus came,
He connected us with the throne through His
divine blood so that we could pray as He did
saying, **Father, I thank thee that thou hast
heard me. And I knew that thou hearest
me always** (John 11:41,42). Do you really
believe God always hears you? If not, then
pray until you can truthfully say that and
believe it. Stop wasting your breath if you
don't believe the Lord hears you. Ask Him
to forgive you for your unbelief so that you
can say without a doubt, "Father, you always
hear me." Don't let the devil talk to you and
tell you otherwise, and he can't unless you
listen to him. Never give him a moment of
your time.

BLESS THE LORD

Bless the LORD, ye his angels, that excel in strength, that do his commandments, hearkening unto the voice of his word (Psalm 103:20). Angels have the strength and the vision of the Almighty all the time. They keep what He has promised them and are completely obedient. Angels listen to the voice of God's Word; and whatever He says, they do. They could let the devil talk to them, but they don't.

Bless ye the LORD, all ye his hosts; ye ministers of his, that do his pleasure (Psalm 103:21). Do you do the Lord's pleasure or what you want to do? Are you a people-pleaser or a God-pleaser? You can only please God through faith, and you must please Him in this final hour.

Everything is closing in now; and the Lord said, **When ye shall see these things come to pass, know that it** [my coming] **is nigh, even at the doors** (Mark 13:29). When something is at your door, it's mighty close. That's why Jesus is at the door of every heart today saying, **Behold, I stand at the door, and knock**

(Revelation 3:20). Are you available, or do you pretend to be not at home? You may think you're too busy or have better things to do; but when you're too busy to meet the Lord each morning at the door, you're headed down the wrong path. He won't tear down your door; you have to open it, and you're the only one who has the power to open up your heart to the Lord.

Bless the LORD, all his works in all places of his dominion: bless the LORD, O my soul (Psalm 103:22). Psalms is the most complete book in the Bible; and in it, the Psalmist blessed the Lord continually.

PSALM 121

Psalm 121 is a chapter of victory. **I will lift up mine eyes unto the hills, from whence cometh my help. My help cometh from the LORD, which made heaven and earth** (Psalm 121:1,2). The Psalmist recognized where his help came from—the Lord. What more help could you possibly need here on Earth?

He will not suffer thy foot to be moved: he that keepeth thee will not slumber. Behold,

he that keepeth Israel shall neither slumber nor sleep (Psalm 121:3,4). God will not allow you to be defeated by the devil, your archenemy and His. He's awake and watching out for you all the time, so you have no reason to lie awake and worry; that doesn't solve anything. If you have any doubts, say, "Lord, let me go to sleep, and please deliver me from any doubt I may have so I can wake up with none." Doubt hinders you, weakens you and robs you of your strength.

The LORD is thy keeper: the LORD is thy shade upon thy right hand (Psalm 121:5). My mother and dad were the keepers of their children, and they did a wonderful job of watching over us with the help of the Lord; but the Lord Himself watches over and cares for you. What a marvelous thought!

The sun shall not smite thee by day, nor the moon by night (Psalm 121:6). The sun and the moon may be a blessing to you now, but that won't always be the case. The book of Revelation tells of the sun burning and scorching people to death during the Tribulation Period.

The LORD shall preserve thee from all evil: he shall preserve thy soul (Psalm 121:7). The Lord will make you gentle and kind and keep you that way in His humility, love, grace and greatness. He will preserve your soul, the part of you that will never die, through the blood of the Lamb.

The LORD shall preserve thy going out and thy coming in from this time forth, and even forevermore (Psalm 121:8). The Lord is there for you now and forever.

CHAPTER 7

The Depths of Faith

Divine faith—you must understand and use it. **But Jesus beheld them, and said unto them, With men this is impossible; but with God all things are possible** (Matthew 19:26). Jesus said that all things are possible, and that includes your case. Some of you may wonder if God can actually work a miracle in your situation because you've never heard of Him doing such a thing in the past, but you must realize that it doesn't matter. God can do anything, and He's proven it again and again. When you really get acquainted with God, you'll find He's not a man. **God is not a man, that he should lie; neither the son of man, that he should repent: hath he said, and shall he not do it? or hath he spoken, and shall he not make it good** (Numbers 23:19)?

God's throne in Heaven is surrounded by the seven Spirits of God—the book of Revelation tells us so. **John to the seven churches which are in Asia: Grace be unto you, and peace, from him which is, and which was, and which is to come; and from the seven Spirits which are before his throne** (Revelation 1:4). Those Spirits are there now, and they'll still be there when the saints arrive. I never learned about them in theological school; but God revealed to me that they are love, joy, peace, longsuffering, gentleness, goodness and faith. The last one, faith, is the one we will study in this chapter.

Faith is so important that it's one of the nine fruits of the Spirit and one of the nine gifts of the Spirit, and everyone is given a measure of faith. **God hath dealt to every man the measure of faith** (Romans 12:3). Faith is also one of the six spiritual senses.

We all have five physical senses; but there are six spiritual senses, the last one being faith. Every child of God has this sense, but some won't use it.

FROM LIFE TO DEATH

The book of Genesis opens with life everywhere. **And God said, Let the earth bring forth the living creature after his kind, cattle, and creeping thing, and beast of the earth after his kind: and it was so. And God made the beast of the earth after his kind, and cattle after their kind, and every thing that creepeth upon the earth after his kind: and God saw that it was good. And God said, Let us make man in our image, after our likeness...So God created man in his own image, in the image of God created he him; male and female created he them. And God blessed them, and God said unto them, Be fruitful, and multiply, and replenish the earth** (Genesis 1:24–28).

God created sinless, healthy souls in His own image; and He never intended for man and woman to ever be sick, grow old or die. They had all the knowledge of Heaven available to them and were surrounded by fruit trees of all kinds. They had everything; but Adam and Eve chose the tree of death, even though the Lord had warned them about it. **And the LORD God commanded the man, saying, Of every tree of the garden thou mayest freely eat: But of the tree of the knowledge of good and evil, thou shalt not eat of it: for in the day that thou eatest thereof thou shalt surely die** (Genesis 2:16,17). Just as God had said, they did die spiritually the minute they tasted of the sinful fruit of that tree.

Because Adam and Eve sinned, Genesis closes with a dead man nailed in a box with no way out. **So Joseph died, being an hundred and ten years old: and they embalmed him, and he was put in a coffin in Egypt** (Genesis 50:26). Joseph's remains would remain nailed in that coffin forever with no way out if Jesus had not come, but He did come as a babe from Heaven with all the divinity we will ever need. Who would have dreamed that such tiny, little hands would hold salvation and deliverance and all the powers of Heaven?

Through divine blood, we can carry the powers of Heaven in our hands, too.

FAITH OR FEELINGS

The Bible teaches, **The prayer of faith shall save the sick, and the Lord shall raise him up** (James 5:15). In Romans, Paul tells us to go from faith to faith. **For therein is the righteousness of God revealed from faith to faith: as it is written, The just shall live by faith** (Romans 1:17). Where is that faith?—in your soul. God's people must live by faith; but unfortunately, many of them live more by their feelings than they do by faith.

Human feelings can get you into trouble, but sanctified feelings are wonderful. You can feel hot or cold, and you can feel danger; but you can't let feelings take the place of faith because feelings create only doubt, fear, frustration, depression and oppression. When you live like that, you're not justified. **Now the just shall live by faith: but if any man draw back, my soul shall have no pleasure in him** (Hebrews 10:38). When you're justified, you will walk by faith instead of feelings. You'll find the footsteps of Jesus, and you'll get somewhere with God. Jesus didn't make His steps in feelings; He made them in blood faith.

Some people live so much in their feelings that they can't even reason within themselves. They'll say that they have no faith in doctors, and yet they'll go to one. That's stupid! Never go to a doctor if you're not going to have faith that he or she can help you, and the same goes with God. Never look to the Lord for help if you don't have any faith that He can help you.

FAITH TO FAITH

Some people will come and get prayed for and feel good at that time. They think they have their miracle, and they do; but anything people get through faith can be lost through doubt or fear. You can't give over to anything other than faith, and God has given me the revelation that this is what happens to so many people.

Jesus always went from faith to faith, faith to victory, faith to miracles, faith to healing, faith to peace and faith to joy. As you journey on in life, you must understand that hope will be your helper until you enter into the all-out faith channel where you can get what you need from the Lord. Jesus promised He would get you well, and He said that your miracle should be a great sign to you. Stop going from faith to doubt, faith to disobedience and faith to fear. Stop going from faith to expecting death and go after life, goodness, mercy, healings and miracles.

The Bible teaches that we're to go from grace to grace. **But unto every one of us is given grace according to the measure of the gift of Christ** (Ephesians 4:7). The grace of God means the favor of God; and when you have the favor of God, you have armfuls on purpose from Heaven. You have His honor, His peace, His joy, His salvation and His baptism of the Holy Spirit. He proved all of this by giving you Jesus, the Healer.

The Bible tells us that God's ways and thoughts are deep. **O LORD, how great are thy works! and thy thoughts are very deep** (Psalm 92:5). The Lord told me very definitely to think deep, and He wanted me to preach it to the people. God wants us to talk about our victories rather than our defeats, about our blessings rather than our despair.

USE DIVINITY

When Jesus was on Earth, He delivered people from oppression. **God anointed Jesus of Nazareth with the Holy Ghost and with power: who went about doing good, and healing all that were oppressed of the devil; for God was with him** (Acts 10:38). This verse refers to those who were depressed and being robbed by the devil, but they were not devil possessed. The devil can't possess the souls of children of God, but he can oppress their minds so much that it makes them think they might as well give up. They're tormented and have no real joy, but that's not the will of God. The Lord came and gave us victory over all of that. The devil will bring bad things to your mind and try to convince you that since you thought about them, you might as well do them; but you don't have to listen to his lies. You may not be sinning, but you're not believing either.

Jesus showed you in the Word of God how He defeated the devil in the wilderness. The devil tempted Him just as He finished forty days of fasting; but Jesus fed the devil the Word saying, "It is written...it is written," and you can do that, too. Of course, the devil will come back; but you can run him off every time. Jesus purposely set Himself up as a target for the devil to prove to you that you can overcome all of Satan's powers through the divinity that He brought. Jesus was a true example of human flesh walking the same paths we have to walk and meeting the same troubles and trials we have to meet.

You have to know without a doubt that divinity is real and that you can use it just as Christ used it. Study how Christ used divinity as very man, not just as very God. Jesus never used any more divinity than what is available to each one of us, and He proved that again and again.

HUMAN FAITH IS NOT ENOUGH

Only through divinity could Peter have walked the waters. Many Christians never consider that Peter actually walked, but that's the part that is outstanding to me. **And in the fourth watch of the night Jesus went** unto them, walking on the sea. And when the disciples saw him walking on the sea, they were troubled, saying, It is a spirit; and they cried out for fear. But straightway Jesus spake unto them, saying, Be of good cheer; it is I; be not afraid. And Peter answered him and said, Lord, if it be thou, bid me come unto thee on the water. And he said, Come. And when Peter was come down out of the ship, he walked on the water, to go to Jesus (Matthew 14:25–29).

Peter used faith when he said, "Bid me come." When the Lord answered, it was the living Word speaking; so Peter jumped off the boat into the stormy waters, and he walked. I don't know how far Peter walked, but he did walk; and he was doing just fine until he let fear take him over. **But when he saw the wind boisterous, he was afraid; and beginning to sink, he cried, saying, Lord, save me. And immediately Jesus stretched forth his hand, and caught him, and said unto him, O thou of little faith, wherefore didst thou doubt** (Matthew 14:30,31)?

When Peter looked at the waves instead of at

Jesus, he began to sink; but, thank God, Jesus had not lost sight of Peter. The Lord heard his voice and knew just where he was on that angry sea. Jesus was trying to use this experience to teach the disciples to use nothing but big faith, the only faith that moves mountains and kills all the giants.

Jesus never taught people to use little faith, which is human faith; but that's all many people have today. Jesus called divine faith big faith or great faith; and He marveled at those who used it, especially those who didn't even claim to have salvation. **And when Jesus was entered into Capernaum, there came unto him a centurion, beseeching him, And saying, Lord, my servant lieth at home sick of the palsy, grievously tormented. And Jesus saith unto him, I will come and heal him. The centurion answered and said, Lord, I am not worthy that thou shouldest come under my roof: but speak the word only, and my servant shall be healed. When Jesus heard it, he marvelled, and said to them that followed, Verily I say unto you, I have not found so great faith, no, not in**

Israel. And Jesus said unto the centurion, Go thy way; and as thou hast believed, so be it done unto thee. And his servant was healed in the selfsame hour (Matthew 8:5–8,10,13).

The centurion showed faith and humility when he said, "Just say the words, and it will be done." That answer thrilled Jesus; and the moment He spoke, the servant was healed. Unfortunately, others who were supposed to be of the household of faith were not using their faith just as many people don't use theirs today.

ONLY BELIEVE

For many years, I traveled week after week in the United States, and many times I'd call for alcoholics and drug addicts to come and receive prayer; but there were people who didn't think I should do that. After one great service, I received a letter from an individual who complained, "You prayed for all the drunks and drug addicts, and they got their miracles; but those of us who are serving the Lord didn't have an opportunity to receive our miracles." Wasn't that ridiculous? The Lord was pouring out miracles all over the auditorium, and He promised them to everybody who would believe.

Jesus said, **If thou canst believe, all things are possible to him that believeth** (Mark 9:23). Any word in the English language ending in "eth" means to continue, so you have to keep on believing; *but some people are in and out with believing, saith the Lord.* They cut God off and tie His hands; but then they'll ask, "Why, God, why?" When you won't listen and obey, there's no need for God to explain "why" because you wouldn't believe it anyway.

Some of you depend so much on human faith, and that's why you don't get things done in a miraculous way. You marvel and think I'm so special; but I just serve a special God, a special Jesus and a special Holy Spirit. The Spirit is the Third Person in the Trinity of the Godhead who lives and dwells inside me. He teaches me and guides me into all truth and brings all things to my remembrance that the disciples were taught from the mouth of Jesus when He was here.

But the Comforter, which is the Holy Ghost, whom the Father will send in my name, he shall teach you all things, and bring all things to your remembrance, whatsoever I have said unto you (John 14:26).

You need to contend for the faith that was once delivered to the saints. **Beloved, when I gave all diligence to write unto you of the common salvation, it was needful for me to write unto you, and exhort you that ye should earnestly contend for the faith which was once delivered unto the saints** (Jude 1:3). Contending for the faith means being able to use it. Don't count yourself out; count yourself in.

Stop thinking about your weaknesses and stop acknowledging that various diseases run in your family. It's true that diseases can be handed down through generations, but God taught me that they should stop with you. The divine blood will cut them off if you'll only believe. If cancer runs in your family, it can stop with you when you get salvation; but you must continue to serve God and believe Him if you want to keep your miracle.

Untold thousands have been healed of all kinds of diseases through this ministry, but I'm not a healer; I'm just God's witness and His believer.

FAITH BRINGS PEACE

How powerful is the faith of God?—powerful enough to conquer all fear. Fear only brings torment, and the Bible definitely states that **God hath not given us the spirit of fear; but of power, and of love, and of a sound mind** (II Timothy 1:7). You can have this mind, and you can have faith and divinity; you can have it all! **Whereby are given unto us exceeding great and precious promises: that by these ye might be partakers of the divine nature** (II Peter 1:4).

Fear comes from the devil, but the faith of God brings peace. **Peace I leave with you, my peace I give unto you: not as the world giveth, give I unto you. Let not your heart be troubled, neither let it be afraid** (John 14:27). How much of the world's peace do you depend on rather than using the divine peace that Jesus brought? The Lord promised He would keep us in perfect peace.

Thou wilt keep him in perfect peace, whose mind is stayed on thee: because he trusteth in thee (Isaiah 26:3).

If you will keep your mind on the Lord, your faith will bring you peace; but the most peace some of you ever have is when you're in the house of God. Why?—because when you're there, you yield to the anointing, to the truth and to the thinking of God; and a good preacher should focus your thoughts on Jesus Christ. He's my favorite person in the whole Word of God, and He should be yours, too.

The Lord will start flowing His peace to some, but then they start thinking about their troubles and tribulations or how somebody in their family died with some awful affliction. They allow the devil to put fear in them, and that's not faith. Faith is trusting in the Lord with your whole heart. **Trust in the LORD with all thine heart; and lean not unto thine own understanding. In all thy ways acknowledge him, and he shall direct thy paths** (Proverbs 3:5,6).

God has promised to direct all of your paths; and when you walk with divinity, you have to walk on God's promises. Your paths will be paved with them; and each promise holds all the power, love, faith and greatness of Heaven. I've depended on the Lord to direct my paths throughout my entire ministry, but some people lean to their own understanding. They may say that they want to know God's way, but it's too late for them to seek God's will after they've already bought or done something. If you want God's help, you need to seek Him before you move on things.

DON'T LISTEN TO THE DEVIL

Faith is safety, not false security. The Lord promised, **I will never leave thee, nor forsake thee** (Hebrews 13:5). Because God is always with you, you should have faith that God's deliverance will be yours. Jesus is our victory over sin and our deliverance from all sickness. The Bible says He took our sins and sicknesses upon Himself. **That it might be fulfilled which was spoken by Esaias the prophet, saying, Himself took our infirmities, and bare our sicknesses** (Matthew 8:17). The Lord says the devil is a thief. **Verily, verily, I say unto you, He that**

entereth not by the door into the sheepfold, but climbeth up some other way, the same is a thief and a robber (John 10:1). **The thief cometh not, but for to steal, and to kill, and to destroy** (John 10:10). Why do you ever pay any attention to the devil when he's a thief and a robber?

The devil can't legally afflict you with the things that Jesus suffered and died for unless you let him. Declare to the devil, "I'm a child of God, and you can't touch me!"

Some of you constantly walk in fear of the devil, but I never tiptoe around him. I say, "Get out of the way, Devil, because here I come!" Jesus taught us that when He was being tempted by the devil in the wilderness. He told him three times what God His Father had said; and when He looked around, the devil had left for a season. **And when the devil had ended all the temptation, he departed from him for a season** (Luke 4:13). Notice, the devil left only for a season. The devil will always be back, but you can be ready for him if you have Heaven's greatest weapon—the blood. Jesus knew the devil, and He knew how to get rid of him. There's power in His Word!

LET DIVINE RIVERS FLOW

When the disciples received the Holy Ghost, Jesus told them that rivers of living water would flow from their innermost beings. **He that believeth on me, as the scripture hath said, out of his belly shall flow rivers of living water** (John 7:38). We have to allow the rivers to flow to us before we can flow them to the world, but some of you don't think about that. You don't realize that the grace, power, love, peace and greatness of God can flow through you to others because you're so caught up with your own fear, frustration and troubles.

Divine rivers of love flow only through faith, and they will flush your mind of all the thoughts that are bothering you. The devil will try to make you think that you can't keep your mind off of bad things, but you can. God taught me that a good thought can always shoot down a bad thought, and those good thoughts come from the Lord.

You have to learn to unload anything unlike

God before you can serve others. Jesus said,
**Come unto me, all ye that labour and are
heavy laden, and I will give you rest. Take
my yoke upon you, and learn of me; for I
am meek and lowly in heart: and ye shall
find rest unto your souls. For my yoke
is easy, and my burden is light** (Matthew
11:28–30). The Lord promised us rest; so I
take my burdens to the Lord, and He never
has refused me.

If you would look upon Christ's hands like
the Lord wants you to, the only burden you
would carry is the one for lost souls. We
must be just like Jesus wherever we go, and
we must serve divinity like He served it. In
times of persecution, we have to stand and be
willing to pay the price rather than running
away because we must know that God's rivers
of love are flowing through us.

I carry the burden for lost souls because
that's the burden the Lord wants me to carry.
I'm here to lead people, to teach them the
truth, to build God's Kingdom and to bring
back the King. Many preachers retire from
the ministry when they could still do a lot

more work for the Lord, and that's sad; but God never gave me a retirement plan. I don't want to stop preaching because I'd be miserable if I couldn't preach and teach the Word of God; that's my life!

FAITH DOESN'T DOUBT

Jesus is our victory and our faith. **For whatsoever is born of God overcometh the world: and this is the victory that overcometh the world, even our faith** (I John 5:4). Divine faith brings deliverance and makes all things possible, if you believe. Jesus said, **According to your faith be it unto you** (Matthew 9:29). Human faith can't heal you of sicknesses and diseases, but divine faith can.

This doesn't mean that we can't seek earthly help to aid in our healing. God has given wisdom and knowledge to men and women so they can help us. However, if you're going to rely only on human help, then Jesus didn't need to come for you at all. But He did come, and He is the only true life-giver.

Real miracles only come from God because man can't perform miracles. There are so-called miraculous things that happen in the human, but they're not really miracles; however, God works through miracle power to perform all of His works. God created the first man and woman, and those were two mighty miracles; and He made the human body so complicated that people can study it for years and never learn all there is to know about even just one organ.

The devil will try to convince you that he can bring you real life, but he serves only death; even his words are full of death. Don't go to his death tree, and don't listen to him because he'll beguile you every time. He'll make sin look so beautiful, but sin is never beautiful when you look at it through God's eyes of faith and love. The devil will make you doubt God's promises, but faith doesn't do that.

God told Abraham that he was going to have a son by Sarah, and he waited for that son for twenty-five years. That was a long time, but the Bible says he never staggered at God's promise. He didn't consider Sarah's age, and she and Abraham were almost 100 years old when Isaac was born. **And being not weak in faith, he** [Abraham] **considered not his** own body now dead, when he was about an hundred years old, neither yet the deadness of Sarah's womb: He staggered not at the promise of God through unbelief; but was strong in faith, giving glory to God (Romans 4:19,20). God had promised, and Abraham believed it.

THE LAW VS. GRACE

Abraham is the father of the faithful. **Know ye therefore that they which are of faith, the same are the children of Abraham. And the scripture, foreseeing that God would justify the heathen through faith, preached before the gospel unto Abraham, saying, In thee shall all nations be blessed. So then they which be of faith are blessed with faithful Abraham** (Galatians 3:7–9).

Abraham didn't come through the Law; he came through grace and faith, but many people don't realize that. **For the promise, that he should be the heir of the world, was not to Abraham, or to his seed, through the law, but through the righteousness of faith. For if they which are of the law be heirs, faith is made void, and the promise made**

of none effect (Romans 4:13,14).

Jesus didn't come through the Law either; He came through grace. However, Jesus brought deliverance for all of those who were under the Law as well as those who were not. **For unto us a child is born, unto us a son is given: and the government shall be upon his shoulder: and his name shall be called Wonderful, Counsellor, The mighty God, The everlasting Father, The Prince of Peace** (Isaiah 9:6).

Jesus came when the Law was still in effect, but He brought the promise of salvation and eternal life. If the Promised Seed had come through the Law, He wouldn't have been able to do any more than the Law did; and the Bible says that the Law wasn't sufficient. **For what the law could not do, in that it was weak through the flesh, God sending his own Son in the likeness of sinful flesh, and for sin, condemned sin in the flesh: That the righteousness of the law might be fulfilled in us, who walk not after the flesh, but after the Spirit** (Romans 8:3,4). Grace came and gave us what the Law could not, but many people won't accept it or depend on it.

Under the Law, only the high priest could go into the Holy of Holies to talk to God; everyone else had to stand outside. God would come down on the Day of Atonement, but there was a curtain that separated that holy place where the Lord was until Jesus changed all of that. When He was hanging on the Cross, the veil in the temple was torn from top to bottom. **And the veil of the temple was rent in twain from the top to the bottom** (Mark 15:38).

When Jesus cried, **It is finished** (John 19:30), He meant that God's whole plan was finished forevermore. Jesus sealed it with His blood, and the devil can't ever break that seal. Now, His message is, "Whosoever will, let him come." **And the Spirit and the bride say, Come. And let him that heareth say, Come. And let him that is athirst come. And whosoever will, let him take the water of life freely** (Revelation 22:17). What a glorious invitation straight from Heaven! It's so easy to contact the One who loves you so much.

Age doesn't bother me because I'm busy working for the Lord. Moses was 120 when he died, and he didn't have to get sick to be able to go to Heaven. He even climbed a mountain right before his death. **And Moses went up from the plains of Moab unto the mountain of Nebo, to the top of Pisgah, that is over against Jericho. And the LORD shewed him all the land of Gilead... And the LORD said unto him, This is the land which I sware unto Abraham, unto Isaac, and unto Jacob, saying, I will give it unto thy seed: I have caused thee to see it with thine eyes, but thou shalt not go over thither. So Moses the servant of the LORD died there in the land of Moab, according to the word of the LORD...And Moses was an hundred and twenty years old when he died: his eye was not dim, nor his natural force abated** (Deuteronomy 34:1,4,5,7).

The Lord showed Moses the land of Canaan, but he never entered into it because God took him to Heaven instead. What a blessing that was for Moses after putting up with the many failures of the Israelites for all of those years.

WAVERING FAITH

The Lord said that if your faith wavers, you shouldn't expect to receive anything from Him. **But let him ask in faith, nothing wavering. For he that wavereth is like a wave of the sea driven with the wind and tossed. For let not that man think that he shall receive anything of the Lord** (James 1:6,7). You shouldn't be disappointed in not receiving when you're not qualified—and self can't qualify you. Only divinity can do that because self just fools and robs you.

Human faith will waver if you don't keep your eyes stayed on the Lord; but when you have divine faith, you will be fully persuaded that God will perform all that He has promised. **And being fully persuaded that, what he had promised, he was able also to perform** (Romans 4:21). I never doubt God.

Faith is not rooted in man's wisdom but in the power of God, and He gives all that power to us. Jesus said, **All power is given unto me in heaven and in earth** (Matthew 28:18). All power is in the name Jesus, but how much do you use that name? The Bible says, **Behold, I give unto you power to tread on serpents and scorpions, and over all the power of the enemy: and nothing shall by any means hurt you** (Luke 10:19).

It took divine power to start the Early Church, and the Church today has to have that same power to keep it going. This ministry is the true Church of the Lord, and that's why it's going all over the world. We live and preach nothing but the truth.

Listen to the Word and don't rely on your own or other people's theories. People today spend too much time listening to talk shows on television or the radio, but they don't realize what kinds of minds they're listening to. Talk show hosts spit out things that aren't true; and even when they're proven wrong, they're unconcerned and continue on to tell some other lie that people will listen to. It's all a bunch of garbage, and many of them act so foolishly as one tries to outtalk the other. They all think they have the answers we need; but if they don't have God, they have no answers at all.

USE THE SHIELD OF FAITH

The Bible tells us that faith stops all the fiery darts of the wicked. **Above all, taking the shield of faith, wherewith ye shall be able to quench all the fiery darts of the wicked** (Ephesians 6:16).

When you throw up the shield of faith, all the devil's darts will fall at your feet; but some of you won't use God's armor, and you get pierced with one of the devil's darts. Then you get hurt by one thing after another, and the devil will even work through other people. Some of your own family members may be shooting the devil's darts at you, but all you have to do is throw up your shield of faith and get off and pray.

When you don't do that, you'll whine about what the devil is doing to you; and the devil loves a crybaby. If I'm going to cry, I want my tears to be ones of happiness and joy; or I want to cry over something that God cries over—lost souls. I have never asked the Lord to lift that burden from me, but I've asked Him to give me all the compassion that He had when He went to Calvary and allowed

Himself to be crucified for a lost world.

Faith is for today, but hope is for tomorrow. Faith says "now," and hope says, "Take courage and get ready to use the promises tomorrow." **Faith is the substance of things hoped for, the evidence of things not seen** (Hebrews 11:1). You first have to see the promises through hope, and hope will give you wonderful vision. It tells you that God will look out for all of your tomorrows and that everything is going to be all right if your soul is well with Him.

BELIEVE GOD WILL PROVIDE

You don't have to worry about the storms if you have built your house on the solid rock which is Christ Jesus. No power can ever destroy Him. **Therefore whosoever heareth these sayings of mine, and doeth them, I will liken him unto a wise man, which built his house upon a rock: And the rain descended, and the floods came, and the winds blew, and beat upon that house; and it fell not: for it was founded upon a rock** (Matthew 7:24,25).

When Jesus was on Earth, He saw all kinds

of sickness and trouble; and He conquered them all for us. Then He promised to supply all of our needs. **And why take ye thought for raiment? Consider the lilies of the field, how they grow; they toil not, neither do they spin: And yet I say unto you, That even Solomon in all his glory was not arrayed like one of these. Wherefore, if God so clothe the grass of the field, which today is, and tomorrow is cast into the oven, shall he not much more clothe you, O ye of little faith? Therefore take no thought, saying, What shall we eat? or, What shall we drink? or, Wherewithal shall we be clothed? (For after all these things do the Gentiles seek:) for your heavenly Father knoweth that ye have need of all these things. But seek ye first the kingdom of God, and his righteousness; and all these things shall be added unto you** (Matthew 6:28–33).

Don't worry about the cares of tomorrow, what you're going to eat or what you're going to wear. This verse tells you to look at the flowers and see that they don't worry about tomorrow—and even Solomon in all of his glory was never dressed as beautiful as one of them. If God will do that for a flower, what will He do for His children? I use these scriptures for myself, and then I use them for others. The Bible is the greatest Book of reality to me on Earth, greater than any of the books that God has poured through me. I'm set apart, sanctified and made holy through the truth in the Word.

TAKE GOD'S WAY

Here is one of the greatest of all things about faith: It will bring you into the divine will of God and separate you completely from the permissible will of God. Don't ever ask me to pray for you if you don't want the divine will of God. I never want the permissible will of God; I work only through His divine will and seek to do His divine will in everything.

Angel and I built this work of God through faith. We were already in debt for our tent equipment when we came to Akron, Ohio; but God had told us to establish Him a work, and we set out to do just that. We started out in a big tent without one member, and then we built our big tabernacle in thirty working days. Later, the Lord told me to build a cathedral for Him. My critics said that I could never do it because I didn't have the money, but Angel and I knew God would provide. We knew we were doing His will.

I listened to God and never ran ahead of Him. When money would stop coming in, I would wait on God because I knew that the Lord would never start anything that He wouldn't finish. If you ever find yourself not being able to finish something, know that it's not God's fault. Either He didn't tell you to do it or you didn't work with Him like you should have. I always work with God, and I wait on Him.

When God finally came to me one day and told me that He wanted His cathedral to be completely finished, He meant business. For the first time in the ministry, the meal barrel stayed full—the more we spent, the more we had; and the Lord told me that the cathedral would be a memorial of His faith and love to all who saw it.

LIVE BY PROMISE

This whole ministry was built by faith, and it's now the platform for the world. It has taken well over fifty years to build it, but it's much more than just materials that man put together. It's built on Jesus, our rock and our solid foundation. **For other foundation can no man lay than that is laid, which is Jesus Christ** (I Corinthians 3:11). Jesus must be your rock, too. In Him, you'll find everything you need for this end-time journey. **O come, let us sing unto the LORD: let us make a joyful noise to the rock of our salvation** (Psalm 95:1).

The Lord is now working in a greater way in this ministry than ever before. In the past, whenever I needed an answer from God and had done all I could do, I would tie a knot at the end of my rope and hang on. Then recently, the Lord came to me in a vision and said, "Let go of the knot, and you'll land on the sea of promises." When I looked down, there was a beautiful sea below me filled with all of the promises of God; and every wave was a promise. I let go, and I could feel myself going down through the air of His blessings, strength and greatness; and I landed so gently on His sea of promises. Then He told me that I would never have to tie a knot in the end of my rope again.

That vision has burned upon my soul, and I've been walking on His sea of promises ever since; and I will continue to walk on it as long as Heaven's voice calls me to duty. God Himself told me that every promise carries all the power of Heaven, so I preach through the promises of God; I travel to the nations and win thousands of souls through the promises of God.

God taught me to depend on His promises when I was just a young man headed for theological school. I never thought I'd attend college until the Lord told me that I was to go, and it was a rough road. It was during the Great Depression, and I didn't have the money to go to school; but I learned that when God tells you to do something, He will supply what you need. **But my God shall supply all your need according to his riches in glory by Christ Jesus** (Philippians 4:19).

I believed that, and faith worked; but I didn't just sit down, fold my hands and expect God to do everything. He gave me the faith, and I had to put that faith into action.

When I first went to look over the school God had told me to attend, I only had about five dollars; but little by little, God did provide the money I needed just as He had promised He would. I learned so much while I was at school because I had been taught the Word of God in public school, and my mind was fertile. Even as a child, I was being made ready for the ministry.

This ministry was built on the promises of God. The great airplane we have that takes us to the nations came through a divine promise, and I waited for it for over thirty years. There was no need for me to ask anybody about it because to man, getting one looked impossible. I had to depend 100 percent on God. He had told me that we would have a plane one day, and I believed it. When that day came, God provided exactly what we needed; and I thank God every time that those big wings carry us to the nations. When I look out the window as we fly, I know we're in God's plane; and I know we're safe in the hands of the One who came with deliverance for all.

A TWO-FOLD ATONEMENT

Christ made healing available to everybody. The miracles and healings recorded in the Old Testament that came through special men at special times were types and shadows of the healing Christ who would come later. Jesus brought back everything that was lost in the fall of man through His suffering and His death on the Cross. It was not just a one-fold atonement but a two-fold atonement. The Bible tells us that Jesus became the Sacrificial Lamb for our physical healing when He went to the whipping post. Then He went to Calvary and died on the Cross for our sins. **Who his own self bare our sins in his own body on the tree, that we, being dead to sins, should live unto righteousness: by whose stripes ye were healed** (I Peter 2:24). Notice that this scripture says "ye *were* healed." This means that Christ has already paid for your healings. They're on the table for you, and you don't have to beg or hope for them.

This scripture also definitely states that when you're dead to sin, you will live unto righteousness; yet people still say that no one can live free from sin. You must live free if you want to walk with the Lord because the Bible says, **The soul that sinneth, it shall die** (Ezekiel 18:4). When you say that you can't live free from sin, you're calling God a liar; and you have no truth. You've trampled His truth underfoot and instead have taken false things into your spirit; then judgment can fall on you at any time. If the Word, Jesus, hadn't come down and given His life, we wouldn't have what we have today; and we couldn't believe like we believe. Divinity is what saved you and keeps you saved.

Divinity is all about love, but so many today are hurting in their hearts and don't know what's available to them. Perhaps you've been hurt in the past, and you didn't have the love as a child that you should have had; but you can have it now. You can use divine love just like I did when Angel passed away, and it will work to heal all of your hurt. Your past won't matter anymore because faith in God will take care of it all. Faith works with love, and love yields to faith; they work hand-in-hand.

CHAPTER **8**

Jesus' Healing Wings

Jesus came to Earth with healing in His wings for every man, woman, boy and girl. **But unto you that fear my name shall the Sun of righteousness arise with healing in his wings** (Malachi 4:2). You must know and understand all that is in those divine wings. We're all familiar with physical wings, and we know that birds and airplanes can't fly without them; but the wings of Jesus are spiritual wings, and they are a force to reckon with. In those mighty, powerful wings we find love, faith, grace and healing. Every feather of those wings is divine—divine hope, divine peace, divine joy, divine patience, divine gentleness, divine goodness, divine self-control and divine meekness.

Consider how powerful the wings of an eagle must be to enable it to rise above the storms. Then compare them to Jesus' wings which have the power to lift us up above all the storms of life and take us to Heaven where there will never be any more storms. There's more strength, more power and more greatness in the wings of Jesus than in any thing or any person on Earth. Those same wings will take us in the Rapture, so why would you ever doubt that it will happen? Doubt comes when you don't thoroughly understand the wings of Jesus and the power they have to change you in a moment, in a twinkling of an eye. I thank the Lord for Jesus' wings, and I love everything in them. Salvation came in those wings, and no one can be born new without them.

JESUS BROUGHT LIGHT
WITH THE GOSPEL MESSAGE

On that great night of Christ's birth, He came on wings of love; but He landed in a barnyard. He was born in an ox stall and laid in a manger with only some straw for a bed. Most of the world didn't realize that He had come to bring **joy unspeakable and full of glory** (I Peter 1:8) and peace for all. The Lord gave me a revelation that in the wings of Jesus came the seven Spirits of God that we studied earlier and much more. He emphasized "much more," and that thrilled me!

Jesus brought hope from Heaven for the hopeless and light to those who were in the night. **The people which sat in darkness saw great light; and to them which sat in the region and shadow of death light is sprung up** (Matthew 4:16). The world was in such darkness when Jesus came; the people had no reality in God the Father, God the Son or God the Holy Ghost. They didn't know what real love was like, but Jesus brought love for all mankind. Suddenly, every child could grow up in grace if his or her parents would accept what was in the wings that brought Jesus to us.

That same divine light is still here now, and it shines greater than ever because this is the final hour. Unfortunately, few people see it because so many who once had the light have turned it out. They want to be like the rest of the world, so they have denied the Jesus who gave everything for them.

When Jesus came, He brought more divinity than we would ever need; but how much of it do you use? Why do you feel that you have to battle so much to use it?—It's because you let fear bind you. You're afraid to stand up tall, and you do more running from the devil than you do trampling him underfoot. You can make the devil run if you'll use the power and the healing that Jesus brought in His wings. **Submit yourselves therefore to God. Resist the devil, and he will flee from you** (James 4:7).

Do you tell the devil he has to go, or do you let him worry you to death? Don't allow him to do that; give him the Word. Some of you never take time to give the devil the Word, so you never get rid of him. Have you ever tried reading the Bible to the devil when he's disturbing you or worrying you? Try it, and you'll find it works because the devil can't stand the Word. Always remember that when the devil came against Jesus, He gave him the Word.

DON'T BE AFRAID OF THE DEVIL

When Jesus was here, He uncovered the devil for what he really is; and He enabled people to see him as He knew him. In the beginning, He knew him as a beautiful angel; but He also knew him after he had fallen and come into his current degraded and ugly state. **He was a murderer from the beginning, and abode not in the truth, because there is no truth in him. When he speaketh a lie, he speaketh of his own: for he is a liar, and the father of it** (John 8:44).

The devil is a liar, so why let him bother you or accept what he says? Don't let the devil get your attention. If a fly bothers you, you'll grab the fly swatter and kill it; but you won't use the blood to swat the devil and get rid of him. You're afraid to disturb him because you think he'll come after you. Well, I have news for you—he's already after you; the Bible says he roams the Earth like a roaring lion. **Be sober, be vigilant; because your adversary** the devil, as a roaring lion, walketh about, seeking whom he may devour (I Peter 5:8).

The devil's growl may be loud and ferocious, but you must realize that he doesn't have power against the blood. Just one drop of divine blood can defeat Satan's whole kingdom. The Lord said, **If the Son therefore shall make you free** [talking about Himself], **ye shall be free indeed** (John 8:36). I use that as dynamite on the devil through the blood. I scare him with blood-bombs, and he runs. He'll run from you, too, if you'll use the blood.

I like to rub the devil's nose in the fact that just one angel with one chain of blood will put him into the pit. **And I saw an angel come down from heaven, having the key of the bottomless pit and a great chain in his hand. And he laid hold on the dragon, that old serpent, which is the Devil, and Satan, and bound him a thousand years, And cast him into the bottomless pit, and shut him up** (Revelation 20:1–3).

You'll be able to look at him in that pit if

you want to. The Bible says, **They that see thee shall narrowly look upon thee, and consider thee, saying, Is this the man that made the earth to tremble, that did shake kingdoms** (Isaiah 14:16)? People will just glance at the devil in the pit and say, "Is that the one who turned the world upside down and caused so much evil? He doesn't look like much." But you won't find me around there; I've seen enough of the devil.

While the Lord was teaching me about the gift of discerning, I had to see plenty of Satan and his demons. The Lord took me right into the devil's kingdom, and I still have to see devils today. When I pray for people to be delivered, God lets me look into their souls and see the devils and the darkness that bind them. People will talk to me and act like they have divine victory; but when I look into their souls, there's nothing but darkness.

Don't back away from the devil; meet him head-on with the blood. The devil runs from the blood because it renders him helpless; but you must be aware that the more the Holy Spirit manifests Himself to you, the more the devil will try to do the same thing. He has tried to fool me in many ways, and he'll try to fool you, too, with his manifestations; he never gives up. I can actually hear noises that he makes, and you may hear such noises, too; but don't let him frighten you. If you hear a noise, first make sure it's the devil; then rebuke him. You can start singing, *There is power, power, wonder-working power in the blood of the Lamb.* Sing that chorus over and over until the devil flees.

CHRIST'S MIRACULOUS BIRTH

The angels were so excited over what was in the wings of Jesus. They knew about salvation, but they couldn't understand it because they had never experienced it; however, they knew it would change mankind. The angels were a part of God's great plan, and they ministered to those who would accept what was in the wings of Jesus the night He was born. When the shepherds saw the star and heard the angels, they rejoiced with great joy; but there was no big crowd waiting to receive Him, and that was such a shame.

Christ's birth had been prophesied for

hundreds of years, yet no one was there to receive the One who had come from Glory. The animals were there; and when I envision them, I see all their little heads perked up and their eyes shining. I see the sheep and the goats coming forth and all the other animals gathering around to witness the birth of the Savior of the world, the miracle of the Virgin Birth.

Jesus brought life; and as I imagine that scene, I see all nature waking up that night. I see the flowers Jesus helped to create leaping up in full bloom. I hear the birds singing the songs of gladness that He helped to write, and the leaves on the trees must have been shouting, "Hallelujah!" I also see an unusual star, and there's no star like the Jesus star. The Lord has let me see it many times, and it has thousands of manifestations. It's fascinating to watch, and my faith goes Heaven-high as I watch it moving inside people and healing them.

MIRACLES FROM GOD

The first miracle of my ministry after receiving the first gifts was for a woman who had hobbled into one of my services on crutches. The people in that place were not used to seeing a lot of outstanding miracles, but they were about to see something far beyond what they had ever seen before. I raised my hand, and the woman dropped her crutches just as if she'd been shot with a gun. She stood erect and was able to move around with complete liberty. She left her crutches right where she had dropped them for the rest of the crusade, and she walked off just as if nothing had ever been wrong.

God worked through this humble servant another time as I held a little, deformed baby boy. One side of his face and head was smaller than the other; but the Spirit of God moved over him like a gentle breeze, and I watched that baby be made whole. Have you ever held a miracle? It's wonderful! Then I had the pleasure of passing the baby to his father. Many people in that community knew that baby boy, and they could hardly believe their eyes. They just wanted to touch him and hold him, and they passed him around like he was a collection plate. There's nothing like seeing the Lord at work. It's worth any sacrifice to watch Him take death out of a person and replace it with life or to watch Him re-create part of a person's body.

In a miracle service in Cuba, there was a little boy about four years old who was crippled and couldn't walk. I prayed for him, and God instantly made him whole. It turned the place upside down, and the people went wild.

One particular miracle touched me in a great way. A woman with a baby came in on crutches; and as I started to minister to her, all she told me about was her baby's affliction—she didn't say anything about herself. I prayed for her baby, and then I hesitated; but she didn't say anything else. Finally, I said, "Don't you want to be healed?" Her eyes got big as she looked up at me and said, "Why, I never thought about it." I said, "You can be healed right now!" Then God instantly healed her, and you've never seen a happier mother.

She told me later that she had come to the service to get her baby healed, and then she was going to take her life. She could no longer take being a cripple and not being able to care for her children. But God moved for her; and when I returned to that same place a year later for another tent meeting, that woman was right there helping my crew carry and set up the chairs. She still had her miracle and was so excited to be able to help.

JESUS BROUGHT MIRACLE POWER

Jesus brought grace—all the favor of God—in His wings. Therefore, since it's the will of the Lord for you as a child of God to be made whole, your healing is within reach; so why should you be afflicted? There are Christians who don't have one sin in their lives, yet they wonder why they're afflicted. You have to fight for your miracle, and everything you need to fight with came in the wings of Jesus. The Lord proved it when He sent His twelve disciples forth and told them to heal the sick. They were told to go from city to city to heal the people and to cast devils out of them... and they did so with great success. **Then he [Jesus] called his twelve disciples together, and gave them power and authority over all devils, and to cure diseases. And he sent**

them to preach the kingdom of God, and to heal the sick. And they departed, and went through the towns, preaching the gospel, and healing everywhere (Luke 9:1,2,6).

Then Jesus sent the seventy, the laypeople, forth. **After these things the Lord appointed other seventy also, and sent them two and two before his face into every city and place, whither he himself would come. Therefore said he unto them, The harvest truly is great, but the labourers are few: pray ye therefore the Lord of the harvest, that he would send forth labourers into his harvest. And the seventy returned again with joy, saying, Lord, even the devils are subject unto us through thy name** (Luke 10:1,2,17). Laypeople from this ministry are going forth in other countries—onto the streets, into the prisons, hospitals and schools—and they're having success in the Lord.

Physical healing is so important to God that He healed all the Israelites, three or four million people, when He brought them out of bondage. God had told the Israelites, **I will take sickness away from the midst of**

thee (Exodus 23:25). Do you believe that with all of your heart, and do you act on it? The true faith of God will show in how much you act out the promises of God in the Holy Scriptures, and you have to use them without one doubt if you want the perfect results that God has promised. When God brought the Israelites out, the Psalmist declared through the Holy Ghost that there wasn't one weak person among them. **He brought them forth also with silver and gold: and there was not one feeble person among their tribes** (Psalm 105:37).

God made a covenant of healing with the Israelites after they had come out of Egypt. **If thou wilt diligently hearken to the voice of the LORD thy God, and wilt do that which is right in his sight, and wilt give ear to his commandments, and keep all his statutes, I will put none of these diseases upon thee, which I have brought upon the Egyptians: for I am the LORD that healeth thee** (Exodus 15:26). *I am the Lord that healeth thee* is one of the seven names that Jehovah God gave Himself for the Israelite nation. That name still stands today for all the sons and daughters of God.

JESUS BROUGHT IT ALL

Hear the Lord saying to you today, "Child, I am your Father who healeth thee." Always accept that and then use it with all the faith that will make it work. Everything else will fade when you use the blood that the Lord is giving us so much knowledge about. I use faith and act out the Word. I don't have to check to see if I have faith; I know I have it because I have the faith manuscript—the Bible—and I believe it all!

When God speaks to me, I move. When the Lord calls me to duty, I lose sight of all people and focus on Him; and like the Apostle John, I see Jesus only through eyes of love. We are truly blessed, but some of you don't feel like you are. I always know that I'm blessed no matter how hard the going gets. I know that the Lord holds all of my tomorrows in His wonderful, loving hands.

Jesus brought a marvelous part of Heaven down to Earth, and it all belongs to you. It had never come in that fashion before; but it cost Jesus His life, and He had to be separated from His Father for over thirty years. He went through such hardships—going hungry, fasting, praying and losing sleep—but He delighted in talking to the Father and doing His will.

How many times have you been glad when your family went to sleep so you could talk to your Father in Heaven? I talk to the Father at all hours, and they're such wonderful times. I love talking to Him in the early morning hours when my mind is as clear as a crystal; it's almost like being in Heaven. It's no wonder that the Lord said, **Be still, and know that I am God** (Psalm 46:10).

In those wings is everything you need; but so many look elsewhere, saith the Lord. I believe in good doctors and hospitals, but I believe in taking a case to Jesus first through the faith that He brought in His wings. Some people don't look into the manger like they should; but I'm forever looking into the manger, the place where I found forgiveness, freedom from all sin and healing for my whole body. Nothing that Jesus brought has ever failed, but the majority of the human race has failed Him in rejecting all that was in His wings of love and by denying His power. **Having a form of godliness, but denying the power thereof: from such turn away** (II Timothy 3:5).

We must realize the power Jesus brought and let Him direct our lives. He moves with wings that carry us all over the world; and we're taking with us His Gospel message of grace, gentleness, kindness, love, understanding, wisdom, knowledge, discernment, truth and miracles. There's no limit to any of God's greatness. The wings of Jesus are the cure for all sadness, weakness and sickness; and they're the supply for all of our needs.

WE ARE BLESSED

Behold the Lamb of God (John 1:29). John the Baptist cried those words more than one time. Is Jesus the Master of all your seas? How much hope and trust do you put in Him? How much do you appreciate each and every blessing you receive from Him, and do you count them often enough to keep you from complaining? If you would stay up for days on end counting all your blessings, I'm sure you'd never be able to count them all. What has the Lord done for you and for those you love? He saved us from hell, and that alone is enough to rejoice over forevermore.

The Bible says there's a mansion in Heaven for everyone. **In my Father's house are many mansions: if it were not so, I would have told you. I go to prepare a place for you. And if I go and prepare a place for you, I will come again, and receive you unto myself; that where I am, there ye may be also** (John 14:2,3). This promise alone should make you sing and rejoice, but many people sing the songs of Canaan without really meaning them or applying them to their lives. Don't sing the songs of the world, and don't listen to anything you wouldn't want to be listening to when the Lord comes because one of these days or nights He is coming.

When God saved me, I stopped listening to the songs of the world. I started listening to songs of the Lord, and I meant every word of the Gospel songs and choruses I sang. They became a part of me then, and they're still a part of me now. They make me happy, and they give me strength for the journey. They brighten my way, dispel the darkness, calm the angry seas and give me power to walk the waters. I love to sing and make melody in my heart to the Lord. **Be filled with the Spirit; Speaking to yourselves in psalms and hymns and spiritual songs, singing and making melody in your heart to the Lord** (Ephesians 5:18,19).

Jesus came loaded down with all kinds of treasures and gifts for us, with freedom and liberty for all. He brought the Year of Jubilee so we would no longer have to be slaves to the devil. **The Spirit of the Lord is upon me, because he hath anointed me to preach the gospel to the poor; he hath sent me to heal the brokenhearted, to preach deliverance to the captives, and recovering of sight to the blind, to set at liberty them that are bruised, To preach the acceptable year of the Lord** (Luke 4:18,19). Thank God Almighty, we're free because His wings brought resurrection power. We can be resurrected from the dead person we once were and be given the life of Heaven.

That life is eternal life, and we have it because of Jesus' love. Human love can give life to a certain extent, but it takes divine love to receive eternal life. The Lord told me that His love dispels all darkness and despair, and it's available in healing from Heaven.

HEALING LOVE

Some of you grew up without love and may even have been abused as children. Your home was full of the devil, and you only heard the name of God and Jesus used in blasphemies. Perhaps you were beaten beyond anything that a human should ever endure, but you won't let the Lord heal you. I try my best to get people to accept God's love. I've gone on many long fasts trying to bring people into one mind and one accord in the work of the Lord, but people have to accept divine love and want to be healed. If people just talk about divine love without using it, they'll carry bitterness; and that's not God's way. The Lord said we should pray for the souls of those who have mistreated us. We don't have to like them; even God doesn't like them, but His blood-love is the only thing that can erase the scars of abuse. Sympathy won't do the job, and that's why Jesus is not our sympathizer—He's our substitute.

Hate nailed Jesus to the Cross, but love kept Him hanging there. He could have called thousands of angels to save Him, but He didn't. He said, **I lay down my life, that I might take it again. No man taketh it from me, but I lay it down of myself. I have power to lay it down, and I have power to take it again. This commandment have I received of my Father** (John 10:17,18).

The Lord said that God has no greater healing than what comes through love. It heals sinful hearts and changes degraded lives that have been destroyed by the devil; then it transforms them into wonderful people. The Psalmist said, **I will praise thee; for I am fearfully and wonderfully made** (Psalm 139:14). That's what love can do. Some of you wouldn't dare say that you were wonderfully made because you'd think you were bragging; but when you say what God says, you're not bragging. You're talking faith, and that's "God-talk." How many times have you thanked God that you're wonderfully made? I can never thank Him enough for such a miracle.

GET RID OF THE PAST

Don't let your past bother you when the Spirit of God can just wipe it all away. Paul said, **This one thing I do, forgetting those things which are behind, and reaching forth unto those things which are before, I press toward the mark for the prize of the high calling of God in Christ Jesus** (Philippians 3:13,14). In other words, close the doors behind you and get rid of the past.

Divine love is a stranger to so many people because they keep looking back. I've watched people down through the years who have missed out because they left the door cracked a little bit. That's dangerous because it means they're thinking about returning. I closed all my doors of the past and sealed them with the blood of Jesus through the Holy Ghost. That seal can't ever be broken, and I'm never going back.

When Jesus was on Earth, He told us to **remember Lot's wife** (Luke 17:32). For just one look, she lost her husband, her daughters, her life and her soul. She loved what was in Sodom and Gomorrah more than she loved her family and more than she loved God. An angel was on each side of her dragging her out; but in spite of that, she looked back. Those two angels were a type and shadow of the Word and the Holy Ghost, and they are what will bring us out today.

Stop looking at who you used to be. You have to erase all of that from your mind, and the Holy Spirit can do it through your obedience. Then you'll realize that you're in the family of God and that the Lord loves all of His children. He's hugging each one just as tightly as they will let Him, and love begets love.

Always look to Jesus; He's not driving us from behind but leading us from the front. It's so simple to follow Him, and His blood gave us all the power we need over death, hell and the grave. **Death is swallowed up in victory. O death, where is thy sting? O grave, where is thy victory** (I Corinthians 15:54,55)? Jesus didn't win for Himself but for all of us, and that makes you a winner if you belong to Him. Do you act like a winner and enjoy the benefits of a winner, or is it just talk and not reality? You have to let all that Jesus brought become real to you.

Even before Jesus came, God and His Son were real to Job. He said, **For I know that my redeemer liveth, and that he shall stand at the latter day upon the earth** (Job 19:25). Job knew the power of his God; and he said, **When he hath tried me, I shall come forth as gold. My foot hath held his steps, his way have I kept, and not declined. Neither have I gone back from the commandment of his lips; I have esteemed the words of his mouth more than my necessary food** (Job 23:10–12).

Job knew that there was no part of the world in him. **Behold, my witness is in heaven, and my record is on high** (Job 16:19). Job knew that God saw everything and that He had a record book up in Heaven detailing the way Job had lived. Job's wife wanted him to **curse God, and die** (Job 2:9); but Job said, **Thou speakest as one of the foolish women**

speaketh (Job 2:10). His wife talked like a sinner, but Job was determined to bless God and live. **The LORD gave, and the LORD hath taken away; blessed be the name of the LORD** (Job 1:21). Although Job believed that the Lord was the one who had taken everything away, he still trusted Him. We know that it was the devil who took Job's things away, but Job didn't have that insight; however, he did have the heart of God, and he won!

FOLLOW JESUS

Job used divinity just as Jesus did, and Jesus came to show us how to use it, too. Do you pattern your life after Jesus or after people? Don't measure yourself against what others do because they may not be answering God's call to duty; and if you follow them, you won't be answering the call either. I don't look at other people as my examples; I look at Jesus. I only want to know what He would say or do, and I wait until He shows me.

You have to know that the wings of Jesus will never fail you. Those wings covered the whole Earth the night Christ was born,

and they still cover the whole Earth today.
Everyone can find rest under those wings.
Have you found true rest, or are you always
frustrated about something? Some of you
always feel like you're not going to make it,
and you'll even be a testimony for the devil
by saying so. Well, if you keep thinking like
that, you probably won't make it; but Jesus
is to be our example, and He made it. He
finished His journey on Earth and even made
it back to Heaven; and if you'll live like He
lived, you'll make it, too.

I come under the divine wings to find rest,
not to be tormented or discontented. I come
to rest in love and grace and to live pure, clean
and holy. Under those wings is where I first
found my passport to Heaven.

I keep my eyes on Jesus no matter how bad
things may seem; I never allow the devil to
block Him out of my sight. I don't lag behind
Him, and I don't run ahead of Him; so I'm
always able to find His footprints, and they
lead me on the right path and draw me to
duty. I can step in His steps without any effort
because He is mine, and I am His. I feel His

sanctifying power, strength and closeness. I feel that oneness that Jesus prayed for in John's Gospel. **I pray not for the world, but for them which thou hast given me; for they are thine. And all mine are thine, and thine are mine; and I am glorified in them. And now I am no more in the world, but these are in the world, and I come to thee. Holy Father, keep through thine own name those whom thou hast given me, that they may be one, as we are** (John 17:9–11).

I've found so much for my life under the wings of Jesus because I've never counted myself out. When I left the world behind, I was happy! But some young people won't leave the world behind, and they're miserable. Some may say they're saved when they really never have been. They've never been under His wings, had His love and enjoyed His grace. They've never accepted the holiness of God, and they'll never see Heaven without it. **Follow peace with all men, and holiness, without which no man shall see the Lord** (Hebrews 12:14).

GIVE YOUR BURDENS TO JESUS

Until Jesus came, there was always a shadow of death. The Psalmist knew about it; and he wrote, **Yea, though I walk through the valley of the shadow of death, I will fear no evil: for thou art with me; thy rod and thy staff they comfort me** (Psalm 23:4).

Jesus took the shadow of death out of our valleys and replaced it with rivers of grace, love and deliverance. He is life; and He said, **Because I live, ye shall live also** (John 14:19). **Whosoever liveth and believeth in me shall never die** (John 11:26). Believe in Jesus and in what He brought in His wings, and you'll have eternal life.

The voice of the Lord is calling to us today—so soft, so sweet and so soothing. There's healing in His voice for you as well as all the help and spiritual eyesight you need. He will make all your paths plain, so stop wondering what the will of God is and stand still and see what He brought. In those wings came the will of God for every person who would ever live on Earth, and you don't have to go anywhere else to find it. If you're troubled about something, just crawl under the wings of Jesus today and unload your troubles on Him. The Bible says, **Casting all your care upon him; for he careth for you** (I Peter 5:7). Get rid of everything unlike God, and He'll replace them with His faith.

CHAPTER 9

How to Receive a Miracle

*J*esus is the miraculous Christ, and His ministry was and still is a miracle ministry; so why are you letting anything hinder you from getting a miracle? Decide once and for all that miracles are real because there's no need to seek for something that you don't believe is real. Then you have to set your time to be healed. Some of you have never set a time; and you strain your faith, using it only in little bits here and there because you're not skilled enough in using divine faith and divine love. When you spread faith out like that, it usually turns into only human faith; and you already know that human faith is too weak to bring miracles from Heaven.

Getting a miracle is as simple as getting saved or receiving the baptism of the Holy Ghost, but some people make it so hard. They try to reason it out in the human, and that will never work because faith has nothing to do with logic; it's a gift from God. Christians have told me again and again that they don't have any faith, but that's impossible. We have already learned that every child of God receives a measure of faith according to Romans 12:3, so you couldn't be a child of God without faith. Believe the Word!

You must know that you have divine faith, even if it's just the size of a grain of mustard seed. However, every measure that I've ever received was much greater in size than that. You have that faith, but you have to use it; and you can spend it just like you would spend money. You know the value of your money and how much you have, and you spend accordingly. You check the price tags so you know what you can afford, but what is the price tag on a miracle?—It's obedience. You have to be obedient in everything.

You can't let anything take the place of the Word of God in your life, but many of you do. The Word is always paramount to me; so no matter how bad things may seem, I look to the Lord and keep on looking until things look good. The Psalmist said, **When my heart is overwhelmed: lead me to the rock that is higher than I** (Psalm 61:2). I've cried, "Lead me to the rock" so many times; and the Holy Spirit always leads me there. He lifts me straight up on wings of love.

FASTING BRINGS RESULTS

Jesus told us to ask and receive. **And I say unto you, Ask, and it shall be given you; seek, and ye shall find; knock, and it shall be opened unto you** (Luke 11:9). We all know how to ask and seek, but then you must knock. The Lord is at home for you all the time if you live right, but you can't be in and out with your devotion to Him; you have to be consistent. This kind of devotion only comes about through prayer, fasting and living in the Word.

Remember the man who brought his afflicted

son to Jesus saying, **Master, I have brought unto thee my son, which hath a dumb spirit…and I spake to thy disciples that they should cast him out; and they could not… if thou canst do anything, have compassion on us, and help us** (Mark 9:17,18,22). And Jesus replied, **If thou canst believe, all things are possible to him that believeth** (Mark 9:23).

The disciples waited until the man and his son had gone, and then they asked Jesus why they couldn't set the boy free. Jesus answered, **This kind can come forth by nothing, but by prayer and fasting** (Mark 9:29).

Somebody asked Jesus one day, **Why do the disciples of John and of the Pharisees fast, but thy disciples fast not? And Jesus said unto them, Can the children of the bride-chamber fast, while the bridegroom is with them? as long as they have the bridegroom with them, they cannot fast. But the days will come, when the bridegroom shall be taken away from them, and then shall they fast in those days** (Mark 2:18–20). Jesus said that His disciples would fast after He was gone; and today, devout Christians do fast. If you don't fast and it's not because you're too sick to fast, then you don't have enough of God in you.

You have to conquer your stomach to be able to fast. Your stomach is connected with your mind, and your mind is connected to your soul; and when the soul is connected with Heaven, you will have an anointing to fast. Sure, you'll get hungry, but fasting is supposed to be a sacrifice. You have to suffer for Christ's name's sake; and when you do, you're giving Him glory, and His faith is yours to use. This Jesus ministry would never have been what it is today if people had not done a lot of fasting, and many fasts have gone as long as forty days at a time. That's a long time to go without eating, but we live on the Spirit of God. Did you know a call to fast is a call to duty for the Lord? It's our duty to fast; Jesus said it Himself, and He practiced it when He was here.

A long fast will make you die to self; you crucify the inner person so he will bow to everything God wants. Stubbornness melts like a snowflake in the sun, and you become a pure and clean vessel with your hands in the scarred hands that were nailed to the Cross for you. Through faith, you can feel those nail-prints in His loving hands.

SPEAK HEAVEN'S LANGUAGE

I know that some of your miracles have been within your reach, but you haven't used your faith to see them as I can see them and as the Lord reveals in His Word. Eat the Word, God's will for you, until you can see and know what is yours; and then you'll act like it. Some people defeat themselves by talking about the details of their operations so much that others could almost perform them. All they really need to say is that they were desperately ill, and God made them whole.

I don't talk about weak things. The Bible says, **Let the weak say, I am strong** (Joel 3:10). If I have a pain, others can't do anything about it; but I know a man called Jesus who can. Stay close enough to Him so you can touch His garment or tarry in the waiting room until He heals you.

Read Psalms, and they will help you to

praise God. When you ask God for a miracle, don't keep begging Him. Instead, praise Him for the answer. Your tongue has everything to do with your receiving miracles because it's directly connected with your heart. *Whatever is in your heart comes out through the tongue, saith the Lord.*

Do you gossip? When you tell things about others that aren't edifying, that's gossip; and it causes God to back away from you. Then the devil can move in and afflict you. The Bible says your conversation should be the same as it is in Heaven. **For our conversation is in heaven; from whence also we look for the Saviour, the Lord Jesus Christ** (Philippians 3:20).

When you gossip, you're not speaking Heaven's language; *and your salvation is vain, saith the Lord.* If you take part in gossip, you're deceived; and you shouldn't ever wonder why you're being afflicted. You're hanging yourself with your own tongue. You seem to have plenty of time to talk about others, but you don't have time to spend with God. You have to take time with God and learn how to wait upon Him if you expect to get answers to your prayers. Jesus said we have to ask to receive. **And all things, whatsoever ye shall ask in prayer, believing, ye shall receive** (Matthew 21:22). You also have to be ready to receive.

It's awful to be around people who talk down all the time. I thought that once people got saved, they were to talk about good things, show love to sinners and have plenty of love for the children of God. The Lord said that showing love to one another would let the world know that we belong to Him. **By this shall all men know that ye are my disciples, if ye have love one to another** (John 13:35).

IDLE TALK IS DANGEROUS

Some of you talk to people in a way that you shouldn't. Never use words of discouragement; those are idle words, and they're worthless. Idle talk doesn't belong in the family of God, and the Holy Spirit backs away from it. The Lord warned that you'd have to give an account for every idle word you speak. **But I say unto you, That every idle word that**

men shall speak, they shall give account thereof in the day of judgment (Matthew 12:36).

The Bible tells you to examine yourself, but you have to do it with the help of the Holy Spirit and be willing to accept the truth. **Examine yourselves, whether ye be in the faith; prove your own selves. Know ye not your own selves, how that Jesus Christ is in you, except ye be reprobates** (II Corinthians 13:5)?

You must speak only God-talk. I immediately took on the language of God when I got saved; and if you get true Bible salvation, you'll speak that language, too. God can only use a holy tongue, and He gives that tongue the wisdom and knowledge it needs; but some people are so deceived that they'll pass God's warnings on to others without applying them to themselves. They say things they have no business saying; they talk to people they shouldn't, and they talk themselves out of what they need...and that includes Heaven. Why would anyone let their tongue send them to hell? Mind your own business and don't say things about other people that you wouldn't want said about you. God hates whisperers because they hinder themselves, others and God. People who have lost their first love will only whisper about their love for Jesus.

I read a story about a woman who would gossip to others about her neighbor's wash saying, "My neighbor's wash is so dingy that I'd be ashamed to hang it on the line. It looks like she just dipped it in water." Later on, the woman looked out and noticed how clean her neighbor's wash looked and wondered what had happened. Then she suddenly remembered that she had just washed her window. For all that time, she had been looking through a dirty window while her neighbor had been hanging out clean wash all along.

A lot of God's people put out beautiful wash, but others need to wash their windows. Jesus said, **Not that which goeth into the mouth defileth a man; but that which cometh out of the mouth, this defileth a man** (Matthew 15:11). Do you ever think about washing your windows?

One day, I was talking to a man who was trying to justify himself for chewing tobacco. He said, "The Bible says it's not what goes into the mouth but what comes out." I said, "Buddy, do you swallow that nasty stuff?" He looked at me and said, "No." "Then it comes out, doesn't it?" Needless to say, that was the end of the conversation. Some people are so deceived.

You can't play with God in this last hour. God told me that He has taken the blame down through the years for many things that He never did, and He's not going to take it anymore. He's going to uncover people so others can see who they really are. Do you want healing for the glory of God or do you want it so you can continue in your disobedience? God only heals for His glory.

SACRIFICE FOR THE LORD

We must have the compassion of Jesus to build God's Kingdom like it needs to be built in this final hour and to make it out of here. When you have that compassion, you will give of yourself. Some people will give of themselves when they have the victory but not when trials come. They may decide to volunteer for the Lord; but before long, they claim that they don't have time or that it's just too much.

I never tell the Lord that anything is too much; I learned a lesson about that from Moses. He told the Lord that his burden was too much and asked for help. **I am not able to bear all this people alone, because it is too heavy for me. And if thou deal thus with me, kill me, I pray thee, out of hand, if I have found favour in thy sight; and let me not see my wretchedness. And the LORD said unto Moses, Gather unto me seventy men of the elders of Israel, whom thou knowest to be the elders of the people, and officers over them; and bring them unto the tabernacle of the congregation, that they may stand there with thee. And I will come down and talk with thee there: and I will take of the spirit which is upon thee, and will put it upon them; and they shall bear the burden of the people with thee, that thou bear it not thyself alone** (Numbers 11:14–17).

God took enough power from Moses to give to seventy men, and Moses still had power left; but was he really any better off? His load was lighter, but he also had less power. I don't want the Lord to take any power from me. No matter how heavy the load, I just ask the Lord to give me more strength and power. If people won't use their talents for the Lord, I want Him to give them to me and then give me the strength to use them.

Angel had so many talents. If she would have had more strength, she would have just done more for the Lord. Before we buried her, the Lord spoke to me and said He'd raise up workers to take her place; and when we counted them a few years after her death, we found it had taken seven people. Angel liked to do things that were profitable to the work of God, and she thought it was so worthless to just sit and watch television. She prayed, fasted and studied her Bible; and she was always working for Jesus.

So many people don't want to give of themselves and sacrifice for the Lord, but that shows a lack of compassion. The Bible

plainly says that it's your reasonable service
to sacrifice for the Lord. **I beseech you therefore, brethren, by the mercies of God, that
ye present your bodies a living sacrifice,
holy, acceptable unto God, which is your
reasonable service** (Romans 12:1). That
means we are to brave hardships and fight the
devil, but it's heartbreaking to see people who
are running so well and then suddenly stop.
Do those other things that suddenly become
more important than God's work bring in
souls? How many souls will be in Heaven
because of you? Do you want just enough
strength to serve yourself and your family, or
do you want strength to take the Gospel to the
whole world? It's time to dine with the Lord
and do whatever the Lord calls on you to do.
Get ready to sacrifice and give of yourself in
any way that the Lord wants you to.

HELP GOD MAKE MIRACLES

The Bible says, **Shew me thy faith without
thy works, and I will shew thee my faith
by my works** (James 2:18). That's a powerful statement! People today claim to have
all kinds of faith, but do they have the divine

faith that Jesus had?   That's the only kind
of faith that works.   How many people have
enough of the humility of Jesus to always say,
"Yes, Lord, I'll do whatever you want because
you're first in my life?"

Do you feel the need of God in this last hour?
Do you feel the need of helping Him make
miracles for yourself and others?   The little
boy with the two loaves and fishes felt the
need, and he put that need above his appetite.
When he gave Jesus his little basket, he didn't
know whether or not he'd have any food at all
that day; but he wasn't selfish.   He willingly
gave up his basket without a second thought,
and his love for the Lord helped Jesus make
a big miracle.

There were 5000 men plus women and
children who had to be fed, but the Lord only
needs something tiny to work with.   **And
Jesus said, Make the men sit down. Now
there was much grass in the place. So the
men sat down, in number about five thousand. And Jesus took the loaves; and when
he had given thanks, he distributed to the
disciples, and the disciples to them that**

were set down; and likewise of the fishes as much as they would. When they were filled, he said unto his disciples, Gather up the fragments that remain, that nothing be lost. Therefore they gathered them together, and filled twelve baskets with the fragments of the five barley loaves, which remained over and above unto them that had eaten (John 6:10–13). Faith is always the answer, and faith multiplies.

Are you close enough to God to help Him make miracles? *You should be, saith the Lord.* Do you talk about God's miracles? Are you filled with holiness and righteousness? Do you talk about the great change that took place in you when you found Jesus, or do you talk about your old life?

JESUS IS ALL YOU NEED

The Bible says, **Greater is he that is in you, than he that is in the world** (I John 4:4). It also says that the Lord walks inside of us through His love, grace and truth. **As God hath said, I will dwell in them, and walk in them; and I will be their God, and they shall be my people** (II Corinthians 6:16).

God walks inside of His true children; and when He looks down from Heaven, He sees His image—they act like Him and talk like Him.

All of this came at a great price, so we must realize that we are not our own. **For ye are bought with a price: therefore glorify God in your body, and in your spirit, which are God's** (I Corinthians 6:20). Unfortunately, some people won't accept that, and they don't really belong to the Lord. They're deceived about who they belong to, and they don't realize that self can't get them into Heaven.

People must see Jesus, but some are too busy looking at others. They always know what others are doing and saying, but they don't know themselves or where they stand with God. If He would speak in an audible voice to some people right now and tell them that they were going to die before sundown, they'd be headed for the altar. One young boy was leaving one of my crusade services, and through the Spirit of the Lord I warned him that he would die; but he didn't listen. He just kept walking; and shortly after he had left, he was hit by a car and instantly killed. That boy went to hell.

You have to decide that Jesus is all you need and be determined to learn everything you can about Him. He came to be an example to all of us when He put Himself under subjection to the same human weaknesses that we have to face. **But** [He] **made himself of no reputation, and took upon him the form of a servant, and was made in the likeness of men** (Philippians 2:7).

If your Bible were to be taken from you, would you know enough about Jesus to still do all the work He wants you to do in this final hour? To know Jesus through His love and compassion is the only way to know Him; and to know Him is to love Him, and to love Him is to do His will. The Lord said that He wouldn't withhold any good thing from those who love and serve Him. **The LORD will give grace and glory: no good thing will he withhold from them that walk uprightly** (Psalm 84:11). When you walk in God's will, He'll give you the desires of your heart. **Delight thyself also in the LORD: and he**

shall give thee the desires of thine heart
(Psalm 37:4).

You have to learn what kind of man Jesus
is. **Jesus Christ the same yesterday, and
today, and forever** (Hebrews 13:8). Study
to know how Jesus works and what He loves.
He said, **Lo, I am with you alway** (Matthew
28:20). If you're not walking with God, then
don't expect Him to be with you all the way
either.

JUST ONE THING . . .

The rich, young ruler thought he had it all.
Proudly, he came rushing up to Jesus saying
that he had kept the Ten Commandments
when he really hadn't. He didn't love the
Lord with all of his heart as the Lord had
instructed people to do under the Law. **And
thou shalt love the LORD thy God with all
thine heart, and with all thy soul, and with
all thy might** (Deuteronomy 6:5). Then Jesus
said to the ruler, **One thing thou lackest: go
thy way, sell whatsoever thou hast, and give
to the poor, and thou shalt have treasure in
heaven: and come, take up the cross, and
follow me** (Mark 10:21). Just one thing was

going to keep that man out of Heaven, and just one thing will keep you out of Heaven, too.

One thing can rob you of so much in the Lord just like it did Martha, the sister of Lazarus. Mary wanted to sit at the feet of Jesus and let her work wait, but Martha was in the kitchen worrying about cooking and feeding everyone. Finally, she said, "Master, tell my sister to get in here and help me." But the Lord didn't do that. Instead, He said, **Martha, Martha, thou art careful and troubled about many things: But one thing is needful: and Mary hath chosen that good part, which shall not be taken away from her** (Luke 10:41,42). Mary was dining on the love of Jesus which was far better than any food that could have been prepared.

Martha was concerned about things that didn't matter or count with the Lord, and some of you have that same spirit. There are times when you think you have more important things to do than go to church, but the day you stay home could be the day that somebody who has your mark on them comes a long way. They may never visit your church again; and oh, God, you will have missed that soul! It's hard for me to get over such things.

One day, Jesus held the world in one hand and a soul in the other hand; and He said that the soul was worth more than the whole world. That's how much value the Lord places on just one soul. **For what shall it profit a man, if he shall gain the whole world, and lose his own soul** (Mark 8:36)? God thinks so much of every soul that in my crusade services, He'll pick out a particular person in a crowd of thousands and deal with that person one-on-one. The great God of the universe will use me to help that person. He takes over my mind, and the angel of the Lord who stands by my side helps me deliver the message that the Lord wants him or her to have. Some of those people may have lived degraded lives and be close to hell, but the Lord delivers them if they yield.

CHAPTER 10

Lessons from Jonah

*H*ow often have you studied Jonah? He can really help you. Although you definitely should not seek to be like him in all of his ways, some of his ways were actually good because when Jonah's soul was right, his mind was right. Unfortunately, his soul was not always right.

In the first chapter of Jonah, the Lord gave Jonah a duty to perform. **Now the word of the LORD came unto Jonah the son of Amittai, saying, Arise, go to Nineveh, that great city, and cry against it; for their wickedness is come up before me. But Jonah rose up to**

flee unto Tarshish from the presence of the LORD, and went down to Joppa; and he found a ship going to Tarshish: so he paid the fare thereof, and went down into it, to go with them unto Tarshish from the presence of the LORD (Jonah 1:1–3).

Has the Lord ever told you to do something but you went the other way? Have you ever tried to run from God? We all did when we were in sin, but I've never run from God since He saved my soul and filled me with the good Holy Ghost. That's why I'm in such fine shape with the Lord. Jonah, on the other hand, didn't want to hear in his soul what the Lord was saying; so he ran from God. His conscience had become so seared that the ear of his soul couldn't even hear the voice of God, and many people are in the same shape today. They have good minds in the world's eyes; but their souls are rotten, and they don't have God. Even their consciences can betray them when their minds get so full of all the fleshly things going on in this hour. Your mind has so much to do with your walk with God.

Mental assent is all many have known in the nations we go to because they've never been taught any other way; but when I tell them about faith, divinity and God's healing power, the devils have to go. Then as the gifts of the Spirit begin to work, they know everything is from Heaven; and they yield and get saved and healed of all kinds of deadly diseases. There are many mass miracles; and when the Holy Ghost falls, thousands receive the real baptism. The Lord promised that the greater works would come. **He that believeth on me, the works that I do shall he do also; and greater works than these shall he do; because I go unto my Father** (John 14:12).

God told Jonah to go to Nineveh and tell the people they were going to be destroyed, but he didn't want to go. He wasn't made out of the right kind of stuff and neither are many people today. When you don't pray, fast and live in the Word like you should, you're probably running from God. Even if you're not, you're still walking away; and that's dangerous. Your ears will eventually get so dull that you will no longer feel the urge to pray and fast at all, and you won't feel the call of the Spirit to study the Word.

GOD MOVES THROUGH DIVINITY

You have to live in divine faith and divine love if you want to get out of here and escape the worst time the world will have ever seen. There's just one door of escape—through Jesus Christ. **I am the door: by me if any man enter in, he shall be saved, and shall go in and out, and find pasture** (John 10:9).

You're being freely offered so much from God in this last hour, but you have to use and share what you receive. Jesus taught, **Freely ye have received, freely give** (Matthew 10:8). Some people don't put enough value on the things of God, but His things are my life. When God's eternal life begins to move within me, it gives me unusual strength. After conducting a service, there are times when God's anointing remains on me in such a great way that I can't go to sleep until some of it leaves. Other anointings are so mighty that they last for days.

God pours out great anointings during our foreign crusades, and it never ceases to amaze me how His gifts work for the people. Through the Spirit of God, I'm able to help take them from mental assent to faith. It's always shocking to the thousands of people attending the services when they realize that they can use divine faith and touch God. Many of them are raised in demonic powers and marked by the devil, but I tell them that they can be free! Then I let them know that they can talk to God any time in the name of Jesus and be healed. God's anointing can clear out all deadly diseases.

During the services, people receive miracles of re-creation; and the Holy Spirit sweeps AIDS from their bodies as if it were just a little puff of ill wind. How marvelous! But some of you won't fight for miracles. Why?—because you don't treasure the whole anointing of God. You have all of divinity available to you; so if you put it on every day, you'll be in fine shape.

GOD WAS AFTER JONAH

Going back to Jonah, we find him on the sea in the midst of a great storm. **But the LORD sent out a great wind into the sea,**

and there was a mighty tempest in the sea, so that the ship was like to be broken. Then the mariners were afraid, and cried every man unto his god, and cast forth the wares that were in the ship into the sea, to lighten it of them. But Jonah was gone down into the sides of the ship; and he lay, and was fast asleep (Jonah 1:4,5). Jonah was so dead to God and without feeling that the storm didn't even wake him up, but the shipmaster did. **So the shipmaster came to him** [Jonah], **and said unto him, What meanest thou, O sleeper? arise, call upon thy God, if so be that God will think upon us, that we perish not. And they said every one to his fellow, Come, and let us cast lots, that we may know for whose cause this evil is upon us. So they cast lots, and the lot fell upon Jonah** (Jonah 1:6,7). The men knew something was wrong; so they cast lots among the crew and passengers to determine who was at fault, and the lot fell on Jonah.

Are you a Jonah today who is running from God and from what He wants you to do? Are you running away from helping in the work of the Lord? Where would you be if someone hadn't helped you? Souls are so precious to God. When He saved me, He gave me a working heart that wanted to do anything for Jesus. I never considered any job too humble.

Then said they unto him [Jonah]**, Tell us, we pray thee, for whose cause this evil is upon us; What is thine occupation? and whence comest thou? what is thy country? and of what people art thou** (Jonah 1:8)? The crew members were experienced sailors, and they knew they were headed for destruction; so they wanted Jonah to tell them why the God of Heaven had sent such a storm after him.

Finally, Jonah admitted that he was running from God. **Then said they unto him, What shall we do unto thee, that the sea may be calm unto us? for the sea wrought, and was tempestuous. And he said unto them, Take me up, and cast me forth into the sea; so shall the sea be calm unto you: for I know that for my sake this great tempest is upon you. So they took up Jonah, and cast him forth into the sea: and the sea ceased from her raging** (Jonah 1:11,12,15).

GOD REQUIRES HUMILITY

When the crew threw Jonah overboard, the Lord had a big whale waiting just for him. **Now the LORD had prepared a great fish to swallow up Jonah. And Jonah was in the belly of the fish three days and three nights** (Jonah 1:17). Jonah had to spend three days and nights in the belly of a whale, and the stink alone was enough to have killed him! If you don't want a whale to get you, you'd better take a lesson from Jonah. His story was so important that Jesus reminded us about him when He was here on Earth. **An evil and adulterous generation seeketh after a sign; and there shall no sign be given to it, but the sign of the prophet Jonas: For as Jonas was three days and three nights in the whale's belly; so shall the Son of man be three days and three nights in the heart of the earth** (Matthew 12:39,40).

The whale definitely got Jonah's attention. **Then Jonah prayed unto the LORD his God out of the fish's belly, And said, I cried by reason of mine affliction unto the LORD, and he heard me; out of the**

belly of hell cried I, and thou heardest my voice (Jonah 2:1,2).   Jonah was so glad that the Lord had heard his cry, and he started to change.   Unfortunately, that's the only time some people pray—when they're afflicted and afraid.

For thou hadst cast me into the deep, in the midst of the seas; and the floods compassed me about: all thy billows and thy waves passed over me. Then I said, I am cast out of thy sight; yet I will look again toward thy holy temple (Jonah 2:3,4).   If you've been shortchanging God, you have to stop. *You have to shape up and get ready to be lifted up and delivered, saith the Lord.*

Finally, Jonah considered his soul.   **The waters compassed me about, even to the soul: the depth closed me round about, the weeds were wrapped about my head. I went down to the bottoms of the mountains** [He had gone that low in the sea.]**; the earth with her bars was about me forever: yet hast thou brought up my life from corruption, O LORD my God** (Jonah 2:5,6).   In these verses, Jonah claimed such ownership with the Lord; but he hadn't done that before. Instead, he had been running from his relationship with God.

When my soul fainted within me I remembered the LORD (Jonah 2:7). The soul is the real person. The body will die; but the soul came from the breath of God, and it can't die because it's eternal. **And my prayer came in unto thee, into thine holy temple** (Jonah 2:7). That's when you get your prayers through.

HAVE NO DOUBT

They that observe lying vanities forsake their own mercy (Jonah 2:8). When talking about miracles, lying vanities are false symptoms. The devil will say, "You have a pain, so that affliction must still be there." The devil is a liar, but some people can't get over false symptoms. They'll get prayed for; but when they have another pain, they think they're not healed. That's not what the Lord said; He said He would get you well, and you have to hold onto His Word.

Don't worry if you have more pain. I had pain after I received my miracle, but I wouldn't confess it to a living soul. Instead, I declared that with the Lord's blood stripes I was healed; and with that in my spirit, the blood flowed. I held onto God until there was no more pain. After Jesus had healed me, I knew what I needed was done. Until that happens to you, you have to hold on with faith and live by promise.

I live in the presence of God, and I never have a doubt about anything. No matter what the devil tells me, the presence of the Lord casts it aside; and nothing counts but God. I've had so many divine visitations when I've been shut away with God, and I'm still speechless every time He comes to me. No matter what He wants, all I can ever say is, "Yes, Lord."

God brought this work of His together, and He is the One who raised it up. This is a 100 percent church of Jesus Christ; we have taken up where Acts left off. The sins of the Romans, the Corinthians and the many others don't apply to the children of God because we're free of all of that. We'll be ready to go when the Lord returns; we just have to bring in the harvest. *Thus saith the Lord, it's ready to be reaped.*

Preachers have falsely taught that there will be a mighty revival in the United States, but America and Canada have had many chances; so there is no great awakening to come. Things are getting worse all the time just like Jesus said they would; and we'll soon be saying, "Even so, come quickly, Lord Jesus!" What a day that will be when we bring the last person up the steps to the Upper Room to be filled with the Holy Ghost, and then we hear the heavenly trumpet sound. We must be working for the Lord when it sounds, helping to bring in the last souls.

PAY YOUR VOWS

Jonah continued talking to God saying, **But I will sacrifice unto thee with the voice of thanksgiving** (Jonah 2:9). Jonah praised the Lord; and I'm always praising the Lord saying, "All is well because I'm living in the promises of God." I've prayed for so many multitudes of people throughout the years, and they have received great miracles; but I always teach them that they have to serve God and give Him the glory. God knows that

I never desire any of His glory for the works He uses me to perform.   Some preachers have a hard time giving the Lord the glory and staying away from the fame and fortune, but money has never been my god.   The only thing I want money for is to take this Gospel to the whole world.   I don't need a lot in this life—I don't have a million-dollar home or even a bank account, but I do have a mansion up in Heaven.   I'm a true prophet of God, but I would never have referred to myself as one until the Lord came one day and told me that I was; and He wanted me to proclaim it to the people.   He said that they would see the miracles, and they would know that I'm a true prophet.

Some of you have such a struggle believing and humbling yourself before the Lord because you don't pay your vows to Him. That even hinders your salvation because you have to work so hard to believe.   Evidently, Jonah didn't always pay his vows to the Lord; but after three days in the whale's belly, he said, **I will pay that that I have vowed** (Jonah 2:9).   What have you promised to do for God? When people get saved, most of them vow to do anything for God; but not all of them follow through, and they don't pay their vows to God. I pay my vows to God, and I'll continue to pay until Rapture Day.

Have you made God any promises that you haven't kept? Do you tithe and give to Him? Have you separated from the world and put Him first, or are you too busy to spend time with God? If so, the Lord is going to be too busy for you when the Rapture takes place; and He's going to be too busy to do the things that you need. You have free choice to do as you please, but I've already used my free choice to decide to take the Lord's way in everything.

Once Jonah had humbled himself, **the LORD spake unto the fish, and it vomited out Jonah upon the dry land** (Jonah 2:10). Finally, Jonah was on his way. **And the word of the LORD came unto Jonah the second time, saying, Arise, go unto Nineveh, that great city, and preach unto it the preaching that I bid thee. So Jonah arose, and went unto Nineveh, according to the word of the**

LORD (Jonah 3:1–3). This time, Jonah went as God had told him to; but he still wasn't thinking right.

JONAH LOVED SELF

When Jonah arrived in Nineveh, a city of over 100,000, he cried to the people, **Yet forty days, and Nineveh shall be overthrown. So the people of Nineveh believed God, and proclaimed a fast, and put on sackcloth, from the greatest of them even to the least of them** (Jonah 3:4,5). The people listened to Jonah's words; and the king made a decree saying, **Let neither man nor beast, herd nor flock, taste anything: let them not feed, nor drink water: But let man and beast be covered with sackcloth, and cry mightily unto God: yea, let them turn every one from his evil way, and from the violence that is in their hands. Who can tell if God will turn and repent, and turn away from his fierce anger, that we perish not** (Jonah 3:7–9)? Jonah had not preached mercy to the people, only judgment; but they humbled themselves before God. Humility is what it takes to be healed, and that's why God wants you to study Jonah.

And God saw their works, that they turned from their evil way; and God repented of the evil, that he had said that he would do unto them; and he did it not (Jonah 3:10). When you humble yourself before God, He will hear your cry; but Jonah didn't want the people of Nineveh to be saved. **It displeased Jonah exceedingly, and he was very angry** (Jonah 4:1). Jonah got angry with God because he had wanted God to kill all of those people and send them to hell, but that's not the love of God. It's bad enough to will one soul whom Jesus died for to go to hell, but to will over 100,000 to go is awful. Jonah only loved himself. He may have had some love for God; but if he did, he didn't love Him with his whole heart.

Do you love God with all of your heart? If so, you have to act it out so that God and others can see that love. Some of your unsaved family members may try you to keep you out of church by purposely planning special events during service times. *Many of them are determined to break your spirit and destroy your testimony, saith the Lord.* Take note of this because God is uncovering your relatives.

And he [Jonah] **prayed unto the LORD, and said, I pray thee, O LORD, was not this my saying, when I was yet in my country? Therefore I fled before unto Tarshish: for I knew that thou art a gracious God, and merciful, slow to anger, and of great kindness, and repentest thee of the evil** (Jonah 4:2). Jonah failed to consider that if God hadn't been gracious and merciful to him, he would have been dead and in hell. **Therefore now, O LORD, take, I beseech thee, my life from me; for it is better for me to die than to live** (Jonah 4:3). What a stupid thing to have said! God should have sent the whale back up on land to swallow Jonah again, but God was merciful. However, I don't know if Jonah ever made it to Heaven because we have no record of him getting right with God. As it was, he only had a slim chance of getting there to begin with.

NEVER GET MAD AT GOD

Then said the LORD, Doest thou well to be angry (Jonah 4:4)? Have you ever been angry with God? Some people will get mad at God for taking a saved loved one to Heaven, but how can you resent God for that? The devil loves to make idiots out of people!

So Jonah went out of the city, and sat on the east side of the city, and there made him a booth, and sat under it in the shadow, till he might see what would become of the city (Jonah 4:5). That's a pouting spirit, and it comes from the devil. Jonah still thought God should have killed the people, so he sat up on the mountain to see what God would do.

And the LORD God prepared a gourd, and made it to come up over Jonah, that it might be a shadow over his head, to deliver him from his grief (Jonah 4:6). It's such a waste of time to cry over yourself. **So Jonah was exceeding glad of the gourd** (Jonah 4:6). Jonah loved to be pampered, and he loved the fact that the gourd gave him shade; but it didn't last long.

But God prepared a worm when the

morning rose the next day, and it smote the gourd that it withered (Jonah 4:7). It's so sad that God could use a whale and a worm to do what He needed, but He couldn't use Jonah for much. The worms and the whales don't have a choice, but God gave people free choice.

And it came to pass, when the sun did arise, that God prepared a vehement east wind; and the sun beat upon the head of Jonah, that he fainted, and wished in himself to die, and said, It is better for me to die than to live (Jonah 4:8). The Lord knows how to put people in their place. **And God said to Jonah, Doest thou well to be angry for the gourd? And he said, I do well to be angry, even unto death** (Jonah 4:9). Jonah was running from God because he didn't agree with Him, so beware when you start running from God because it means you don't agree with Him either.

Then said the LORD, Thou hast had pity on the gourd, for the which thou hast not laboured, neither madest it grow; which came up in a night, and perished in a night:

And should not I spare Nineveh, that great
city, wherein are more than sixscore thousand [120,000] persons that cannot discern
between their right hand and their left
hand; and also much cattle (Jonah 4:10,11)?
God had spoken the last word, and He didn't
give Jonah any more room to talk. I wonder
whether or not He ever heard Jonah's voice
again. If He did, Jonah would have had to
have put on sackcloth, gotten down in the
ashes and completely humbled himself before
God.

DON'T BE A JONAH

*You need to study the book of Jonah, saith
the Lord.* It contains many lessons that will
help some of you come out of the states that
you are in. That book sheds God's light on
disobedience and why some find themselves
in the belly of the whale. God wants to
straighten people out so they will humble
themselves before Him.

Some of you have trouble in your marriage
because you have a stubborn streak just like
Jonah did, and God can't bring you out of the
things you're in. If you don't get rid of your

stubbornness, it will one day send you straight to hell. You have to humble yourself before the Lord and ask Him, "Do I have any of the spirit of Jonah in me?" If you do, you can't be a bright and shining light for God.

A child of God is to be like a city shining on a mountaintop for the whole world to see. **Ye are the light of the world. A city that is set on an hill cannot be hid** (Matthew 5:14). I always have a smile for the Lord, and I never tell people my burdens or my troubles. I don't have to depend on other people to be steadfast and unmovable because my raft isn't tossed with the waves of the angry sea. My spiritual anchors hold my raft firm, and I don't ever have to be afraid. I can get off of my raft and walk the waters with Jesus any time.

I love walking the waters with Jesus; and wherever He leads me, I will go. It's like Heaven on Earth for me to be where He is; and when you're in His will, you'll be where He is, too. You'll always find Jesus in the will of the Father. Hide that statement in your heart.

CHAPTER 11

What Hinders You?

What hinders you from receiving from God? For some of you, it's the fact that you don't really believe; and God wants you to know it. He said you just give mental assent, which means your mind may be agreeing with what you want; but your soul is not joining it. *You have to get rid of mental assent because it's hindering you, saith the Lord.*

Mental assent is not faith, and you must be able to separate the two. Some of you would have already received your miracle if you had believed with more than just mental assent. Using mental assent is just temporary—all the devil has to do is make one negative statement, and it dries up. *Then you receive no miracle, saith the Lord.*

You can only deal with God through divinity, and that's why God is not the reality to some of you that He desires to be. But if you've been re-created in God's holiness and righteousness, He should be real to you. The Bible declares, **And that ye put on the new man, which after God is created in righteousness and true holiness** (Ephesians 4:24). Jesus' love will give you the image of God so that when God looks at you, He will see Himself just like you would see the reflection of yourself in a good mirror. For 4000 years, God saw His image in only a very few people. He destroyed an entire civilization with a flood and saved just eight souls because they were the only ones with the image of God. The Lord will never destroy His image; only willful sin can do that.

When you truly have the image of God, you can use the praise cure. That's the greatest cure there is, but some of you won't use it. I receive so much from God for people throughout the world because I use the praise cure, and you can, too; but it has to come from your heart and soul, not from your mind. People live in their minds before they find Jesus; but after receiving salvation, they must live through divinity. Their souls must hear what the Spirit is saying, and the book of Revelation tells us that seven times. **He that hath an ear, let him hear what the Spirit saith** (Revelation 2:7,11,17,29;3:6,13,22). John the Revelator got this directly from Jesus; and if you'll listen to the Spirit, it will make all the difference in your life.

LISTEN TO THE LORD

To receive a miracle, you have to do whatever God tells you to do; but you first have to take time to listen to Him so you'll know what He wants. Jesus' mother helped to make the first miracle in the ministry of Christ when she told the servants, **Whatsoever he saith unto you, do it** (John 2:5). God always gives such simple instructions that many times intellectuals think His instructions are beneath them. You have to humble yourself and bow as low as Jesus did to receive the greatness of the Lord. If you bow to divine humility, you'll be clothed in it; but if you don't bow, you won't ever have it. Doing whatever God tells you to do is the secret to receiving all of the miracles you need. I always do whatever the Lord tells me to do, and I say what He tells me to say.

This is an hour of battles of the mind. The devil will talk to anyone who will listen, and he'll talk you out of every touch of God that he can. He'll make you think you're nothing; but when you belong to Jesus, Heaven counts you as something great. On the other hand, God considers the devil to be nothing but trash; and he serves only junk.

The Lord keeps taking me back to the tongue. Some people talk too much, and they talk themselves right out of so many blessings. The Bible says, **Study to be quiet** (I Thessalonians 4:11). Are you sober before God or do you always carry on with a light spirit and think you're funny? The joy of the Lord is a pleasure to God, but He doesn't like foolishness. When I was young, I was always cutting up with a lot of foolishness;

but when the Lord saved me, He sobered me completely, and I became a different person. I started living in His presence, and I was always thankful for all that God gave me; and I always had an appetite for more. My cry was and still is, "Give me more of Jesus, more of the Holy Spirit, more of the blood, more vision of this end-time hour and more of the truth!"

As children of God, we're supposed to talk like Jesus talked when He was here on Earth. People will recognize Jesus in you by your speech, and it's not so much what you say but what you don't say that gets to them and convicts them. So many people are full of fear, use bad words and always talk about their doubts and frustrations; but you can be a breath of fresh air or a drink of cool water in the desert to them by talking like Jesus talks. That's why you must think before you ever say anything to anybody.

LIVE LIKE JESUS

I want the Lord to be pleased with the life that flows through me because He gave it to me. I live at the tree of life, and that tree lives in me—the name of that tree is Jesus. With that tree come the other nine spiritual fruit trees of love, joy, peace, longsuffering, gentleness, goodness, faith, meekness and temperance; they're all that we need.

The Bible tells us that Jesus understands all that we go through. **For we have not an high priest which cannot be touched with the feeling of our infirmities; but was in all points tempted like as we are, yet without sin** (Hebrews 4:15). Jesus took our pain, our sorrows and our heartaches; but you have to realize this and believe it. **Surely he hath borne our griefs, and carried our sorrows** (Isaiah 53:4).

God is so merciful, and the Bible emphasizes again and again that His mercy endures forever. **O give thanks unto the LORD; for he is good: for his mercy endureth forever** (Psalm 118:29). You have to endure with that mercy or it won't serve you.

You can't sacrifice unto God with a grumbling spirit because it can hinder God from blessing you. Grumbling and complaining can even cause Jesus to back off and prevent

Him from making you whole. However, I want to emphasize again that it doesn't mean you're doing something wrong if you haven't yet been made whole. If you're believing and living holy, then just step forward, believe and be made whole all over. Don't ask God for just one thing; take everything you need.

Some people are afraid that the Lord doesn't love and care for them as much as He does others or that He's going to let them die with some disease. They may think they're doing the best they can, but are they doing the best that the Spirit can do? We have to turn ourselves over to the Holy Spirit so we can live in, walk in and use divinity. He came to guide us into all truth.

Do you use divinity like Christ did or do you put Him in a different classification from yourself? You shouldn't do that if you're truly born new because you're in the family of God, and divinity is yours to use just like Christ used it when He was on Earth.

Some people will knowingly listen to preachers who don't teach the truth, but I don't want to hear what the devil says through them. Jesus didn't want to hear the devil or his demons, and He commanded them to shut up. **And in the synagogue there was a man, which had a spirit of an unclean devil, and cried out with a loud voice, Saying, Let us alone; what have we to do with thee, thou Jesus of Nazareth? art thou come to destroy us? I know thee who thou art; the Holy One of God. And Jesus rebuked him, saying, Hold thy peace, and come out of him. And when the devil had thrown him in the midst, he came out of him, and hurt him not** (Luke 4:33–35).

LEAVE THE WORLD BEHIND

You have to separate. **Wherefore come out from among them, and be ye separate, saith the Lord, and touch not the unclean thing; and I will receive you** (II Corinthians 6:17). Divine separation is the most wonderful thing that can happen to a human being, but you have to completely separate from all ungodliness and from unsaved friends and family. The Bible says, **Love not the world, neither the things that are in the world. If any man love the world, the love of the**

Father is not in him (I John 2:15).

When I got saved, I left the world behind. God made me a brand-new creature because I surrendered everything to Him—the world's music, the dance floor, sports and worldly entertainment. I left the world's ways, its talk and its walk; and I never desired it or ran after it again.

Therefore if any man be in Christ, he is a new creature: old things are passed away; behold, all things are become new (II Corinthians 5:17). If you still love the things of the world—if you listen to its music and go to its places of entertainment—then you're a lover of pleasure more than a lover of God. So many are like that on Earth today because they haven't been made new.

My brother Judd and I had always run around together, but that stopped when I got saved. He knew I had changed, and he never asked me to go anywhere with him again. We still shared the same room and slept in the same bed, but I was a different brother. I no longer argued or fought with him, and that was a miracle in itself because Judd and I had fought

more than any of the other children. I know
he must have been amazed to hear me calling
out his name in prayer each night saying, "Oh,
God, save Judd." But I was determined that
he wouldn't go to hell. I never preached to
him, but I held on to God for him.

Judd had a great love for our dad, and he
thought there was nobody else in the whole
world like him; so when Daddy died, Judd's
hard heart finally softened. As he looked into
the casket, I heard him say through his tears,
"Daddy, I'll see you in Heaven." Later, I won
Judd for the Lord, and he's in Heaven today.

You need to stand up and say that you don't
want to hear what the world has to say. Don't
go where others go or act as they do. You
have to separate yourself into the glory of the
Lord and into the will of God or you won't
have the fellowship you must have to walk
with Jesus.

If you really want true fellowship with Jesus,
you can't socialize with people who won't
live right no matter who they are. You may
even need to stay away from your own blood
kin. Open the Bible and see what God thinks

about your family members. The Lord said He didn't come to bring peace but a sword; He came to separate right from wrong. **Think not that I am come to send peace on earth: I came not to send peace, but a sword. For I am come to set a man at variance against his father, and the daughter against her mother, and the daughter in law against her mother in law. And a man's foes shall be they of his own household** (Matthew 10:34–36).

Jesus has let some of you know about your family, yet you won't separate; but if you miss Heaven, you'll wish you had listened. There's a boy in hell today because he wouldn't listen. He was one of my relatives, and I told him he was going to die; but he wouldn't believe me. God was giving him one last chance, and I pleaded with him with all that was within me but to no avail. Just about thirty days after that, he dropped into hell. When I heard he was gone, I thought, "Oh, my God, just like the rich man, he lifted up his eyes in hell; and he'll be there as the eternal ages roll." He knew the right way; but he arrogantly claimed, "I don't believe like you believe."

When you don't believe what God is saying, He can't reason with you. That's why some parents can't reason with their children— because their children don't believe them. We trusted our parents. If they promised us something, we knew we would get it. My parents didn't lie, and God doesn't lie either.

LET GOD WORK FOR YOU

Paul is one of my favorite characters in the Bible. I marvel at him, and I believe everything he wrote and did because I know that he depended completely on God. Paul had such liberty in the Lord, and we're supposed to have it, too. Liberty is freedom and grace; and when you have them, you have the divine favor of God.

God has used Paul again and again to bring me to where I am today because, like Paul, I have never counted myself worthy to be used of God like He uses me. I never dreamed that an angel would stand by my side, that I could know the thoughts of God on His throne or that He'd use my mind as His very own. I never knew He would give me all the revelations and visions that He does.

I love God and His Word, and I want all that He can pour through me. When God told me that He would pour Himself through His people like rivers of living water, I believed it; and His divinity is now flowing. He told me it would start as streams and creeks and then become rivers and finally turn into seas of water that would cover the whole world. After that, He said Jesus would come. I want to evangelize the world with divine, living waters.

God wants the Bride to be healthy in every way so she will have nothing to fear or worry about. *Thus saith the Lord, He's going to be healing the members of the bridal company more and more.* God wants His children to be happy, and He gives us so much strength when we have the fruit of joy. **The joy of the LORD is your strength** (Nehemiah 8:10).

If you're a child of God and you're not happy, it's because you let the devil hinder you. I'm a happy person, and my only desire is to win souls. I'm satisfied with my calling, and I intend to fulfill it to its fullest with the

help and grace of God just as Jesus fulfilled
His mission.

JESUS, THE HEALER

**And Jesus went about all Galilee, teaching
in their synagogues, and preaching the gospel of the kingdom, and healing all manner
of sickness and all manner of disease among
the people. And his fame went throughout
all Syria: and they brought unto him all sick
people that were taken with divers** [different
kinds of] **diseases and torments, and those
which were possessed with devils, and those
which were lunatic, and those that had the
palsy; and he healed them** (Matthew 4:23,24).
Jesus did all of this before the Holy Ghost was
made available to everybody; but because the
Holy Ghost is now available to every child of
God, just think about what He will be able to
do through and for the Bride.

There's no one like Jesus with all of His
mercy, His tender care and His compassion.
That's why He spent so much time healing
people. **And Jesus went forth, and saw a
great multitude, and was moved with compassion toward them, and he healed their**

sick (Matthew 14:14). Jesus healed through compassion, and we must have that same compassion. Do you have the compassion of Jesus for others? Would you heal people if you could? Would you take away their pain if you had the power as a human being to do so?

I seek night and day to be just like Jesus, and I take a fresh anointing for every miracle service. You should do the same—take a great anointing for every church service you attend and be ready to receive anything that the Lord has for you. Then give Him all the honor and praise.

The Lord heals all manner of sicknesses and diseases, but He doesn't heal all manner of people. He will perform divine miracles and healings when we accept His Word and act on it through the faith of God; but when Jesus was here, He found no faith in His own country. **And he** [Jesus] **went out from thence, and came into his own country; and his disciples follow him. And when the sabbath day was come, he began to teach in the synagogue: and many hearing him were astonished, saying, From whence** hath this man these things? and what wisdom is this which is given unto him, that even such mighty works are wrought by his hands? Is not this the carpenter, the son of Mary, the brother of James, and Joses, and of Juda, and Simon? and are not his sisters here with us? And they were offended at him. But Jesus said unto them, A prophet is not without honour, but in his own country, and among his own kin, and in his own house. And he could there do no mighty work, save that he laid his hands upon a few sick folk, and healed them. And he marvelled because of their unbelief (Mark 6:1–6).

Study Jesus after He started His ministry, and you'll always find Him healing somebody, on His way to heal somebody or coming back from healing somebody. Jesus was in the healing business, and He still is today. It's wonderful for Jesus to heal you, and God's a part of that, too. Jesus said the people would know the Father had sent Him by His works. **But I have greater witness than that of John: for the works which the Father hath**

given me to finish, the same works that I do, bear witness of me, that the Father hath sent me (John 5:36).

The Lord has given me the healing ministry, but I never want people to look at me as the healer. When you go to the hospital, you don't consider the instruments the doctor uses to work on you; you consider the doctor. So when you're receiving from Heaven, know that Jesus is the great Physician and that I'm just an instrument made of clay that God has chosen to use. I know that without Him, I am nothing; and I'm delighted to have Him living in me. **I am crucified with Christ: nevertheless I live; yet not I, but Christ liveth in me** (Galatians 2:20).

MODERN-DAY MIRACLES

When people believe, God can do anything! Consider this amazing miracle: **Then saith he** [Jesus] **to the man, Stretch forth thine hand. And he stretched it forth; and it was restored whole, like as the other** (Matthew 12:13). Today, we're witnessing fabulous miracles like this on all of our crusade trips; and we're bringing people into the Jesus

Kingdom with signs, wonders and miracles. I've ministered to people whose minds were completely gone, and the Lord has restored them. In one city, a father brought his young, crippled son who had never walked and couldn't even stand by himself. The father held his son throughout the service; but after praying for the boy, I told the father to let him go. When he did, the boy not only walked, he jumped and ran! The father was amazed, and he couldn't get over the joy of it all.

In a different city, there was a cute, little guy who was about three; and he couldn't walk either. I prayed for him and for his mother, but she held him tight and wasn't about to let him go. She said, "He can't walk." I said, "He can now." So I took his hand, and he walked back and forth across the platform with me like a little soldier. He was so proud of himself, and I'm sure God marked that little guy just as He had marked me as a child.

The Bible says that great multitudes followed Jesus, and great multitudes follow us on foreign soil, too, because the Lord is pouring out His power just as He promised

He would. **And it shall come to pass afterward, that I will pour out my spirit upon all flesh; and your sons and your daughters shall prophesy, your old men shall dream dreams, your young men shall see visions: And also upon the servants and upon the handmaids in those days will I pour out my spirit** (Joel 2:28,29).

We're living in the last days, and you can have whatever you need. Get ready to be made whole! If you've had an organ of your body removed or were born without one of your organs, get ready for God to replace it. Don't be disappointed and think that it can't happen; just praise God for the miracle. Don't look at the impossibilities; look at the possibilities! See with God's eyes and hear with His ears. The ear to the soul is really the ear of God, so your soul can hear things that your mind can't.

Jesus delivered those who were possessed with devils. **Then was brought unto him one possessed with a devil, blind, and dumb: and he healed him, insomuch that the blind and dumb both spake and saw**

(Matthew 12:22). Medical science can't identify demonic spirits and powers; but God has given me the Jesus ministry, and I work the way He worked. I use divinity; and I command the blind, deaf and mute spirits to go! These afflictions are caused by spirits; and when those spirits leave, the evidence is victory!

There's no sickness in Heaven, just life everywhere; and it won't be long until we'll be there. Rapture Day is just ahead, and Heaven no doubt is already prepared for the one flight out; and the saints will soon be shouting! But until then, we must win souls. **I say unto you, that likewise joy shall be in heaven over one sinner that repenteth, more than over ninety and nine just persons, which need no repentance** (Luke 15:7). The angels rejoice over every soul, and we must keep Heaven busy all the time.

It's hard to tell how many tens of thousands of people this ministry reaches each week; and shortly, the fire of the Holy Ghost will be falling all over the world. The Lord promised me that even those in the upper class would receive the Holy Ghost, and God has gifted me to call the Spirit down upon people. I'm a Holy Ghost preacher; and people are already receiving the Holy Ghost through our CDs, magazines, books, television programs and website—and it's going to keep getting greater and greater.

When I was young, people seeking the Holy Ghost always fascinated me; and I'll never forget the first time I heard the Holy Ghost speak. It was in a little church I was visiting with my uncle, and the Spirit fell on a little lady sitting at the piano. Suddenly, she threw both hands in the air, and the Holy Ghost poured out of her. I didn't know what was happening at the time, but it had such a sobering power to it. That woman is no doubt in Heaven today and has been there for a long time. It's always marvelous to see people receive the Holy Ghost and to hear Him speak! God was real to me as a child, and He's still real to me today; and He must be real to you, too, if you want all that God has for you.

Lift up your hands before the Lord and be

made whole. Know that the Lord loves you, and let Him put His loving arms around you just like He put His loving arms around me. Let Him breathe upon you, and healing will be yours. Don't make it hard when it's so simple.

CHAPTER 12

You Can Be Made Whole

*T*his book has covered so much about God's miracles and healings, and now you must decide that you can be made whole. Jesus asked a man who had been afflicted for thirty-eight years, "Wilt thou be made whole?" **Now there is at Jerusalem by the sheep market a pool, which is called in the Hebrew tongue Bethesda, having five porches. In these lay a great multitude of impotent folk, of blind, halt, withered, waiting for the moving of the water. For an angel went down at a certain season into the pool, and troubled the water:**

whosoever then first after the troubling of the water stepped in was made whole of whatsoever disease he had. And a certain man was there, which had an infirmity thirty and eight years. When Jesus saw him lie, and knew that he had been now a long time in that case, he saith unto him, Wilt thou be made whole (John 5:2–6)?

These words of Jesus prove that you can be made completely whole. Study Jesus and you'll find that whenever He healed a person, He healed them of everything. That's a powerful thought; but as you continue to search the scriptures for yourself, you'll find out that it is absolutely true. And the same is true today—when God's healing power goes into your body, you can be healed of everything; but you don't usually receive any more than you will accept.

THE POURING-OUT TIME

I accepted everything the night God healed me, and that miracle meant life to me. That's why I carry the power of miracles to people all over the world. We are now in the latter rain, the time of the outpouring of the Holy

Spirit; and in my overseas crusades, I've seen the latter rain pouring down like physical rain before me. I've seen it flow in like mighty rivers to cover the people, and I've watched them be made whole all over.

I've watched devils go out of people, and I've seen the Lord and the Holy Spirit take them away like defeated armies. The Lord lets me see devils just like you see people, and they're awful to look at. In some services, the air is so filled with demons that it looks just like a tornado. The Bible declares that the devil is the prince of the air, but he's going to be robbed of that title during the Tribulation Period. **And the great dragon was cast out, that old serpent, called the Devil, and Satan, which deceiveth the whole world: he was cast out into the earth, and his angels were cast out with him. And I heard a loud voice saying in heaven, Now is come salvation, and strength, and the kingdom of our God, and the power of his Christ: for the accuser of our brethren is cast down, which accused them before our God day and night** (Revelation 12:9,10).

Jesus is asking you today, *Wilt thou be made whole?* It can happen in an instant just as it happened to me. The Lord spoke, and it was done. I knew I was going to live, and I wanted to shout it from the mountaintops! I was going to preach the Gospel of Jesus Christ to the world!

WHAT IS YOUR WILL?

Wilt thou be made whole?—I want you to consider every word in this question. First look at the word *wilt*. What is your will? Do you will to be made completely whole or do you just want the pain to leave? Some people aren't interested in being delivered completely; but I accepted my great miracle all over, and I never doubted it. Everything was done, and I knew it. I knew it was the will of the Lord for me to be completely well because the Word declares it again and again.

There are people who have been made whole, but they failed to accept it. They walked away after prayer without realizing what they had received and didn't claim it. If somebody gives you a gift, you can't take it with you unless you reach out for it and accept it; and even then, you can't use it if it's not real to you.

Do you truly will to be healed? Do you will to get rid of all of your sicknesses and diseases? Do you believe that only good and perfect gifts come from Heaven? Will you accept being made whole?

Whether you "will" or you "don't will" is up to you. People may not realize it; but some actually come before God and say in their spirit, "I will not be made whole." To look right into the face of God in a miracle service or while God's message is going forth on television, over the Internet or through the written Word and to have such an attitude is terrible. Some people act it out whether they actually say it or not. They do not believe they can be made whole, and they might as well face it.

Some people will not only let you know that they don't believe, but they'll also brag about it. They're proud to be an infidel or an agnostic, but there are no unbelievers in hell—all who go there become believers the moment they arrive. People may say, "I don't believe

God will send me to hell." No, He won't; but their sins will send them there. God told the Israelites, **But your iniquities have separated between you and your God, and your sins have hid his face from you, that he will not hear** (Isaiah 59:2). Sin separates people from God.

ACCEPT GOD'S GREATNESS

God gave this book to help you come into His greatness and to decide that you can be made whole. You had to decide you could be saved before you could get saved, and you had to decide that the Holy Ghost baptism was for you before you could receive the gift of the Holy Ghost.

At the pool of Bethesda, Jesus healed the only man who believed Jesus in his heart when He spoke to him. The man didn't know who Jesus was; but he evidently had an obedient heart because when Jesus told him to take up his bed and walk, he did. **And immediately the man was made whole, and took up his bed, and walked: and on the same day was the sabbath. The Jews therefore said unto him that was cured, It is the sabbath**

day: it is not lawful for thee to carry thy bed. He answered them, He that made me whole, the same said unto me, Take up thy bed, and walk. Then asked they him, What man is that which said unto thee, Take up thy bed, and walk? And he that was healed wist not who it was: for Jesus had conveyed himself away, a multitude being in that place (John 5:9–13).

That man was Jewish; and he knew that according to the Law, he wasn't supposed to carry a bed on the Sabbath day. But when the critics questioned him, he said, "I don't know who He was; but the One who made me whole told me to carry my bed, and I'm carrying it." Jesus didn't remain a stranger to this man; Jesus found him later and said, **Behold, thou art made whole: sin no more, lest a worse thing come unto thee** (John 5:14). All of the man's sickness was gone.

Later, the man faced the crowd declaring, "It was Jesus who made me whole, and He can make you whole, too." People must believe this for themselves if they expect to receive.

ANYTHING FOR GOD

God doesn't stop with only wanting us to believe; He wants us to go on and say, "Lord, what would you have me to do?" That's an obedient heart. From the time God saved me, I said, "Anything, Lord." It didn't matter what it was as long as I was doing it for the Lord. Whenever they called on me at church, I was ready. If somebody was scheduled to speak in a youth service and they didn't want to, I'd do it. When they had to jack up the church building, I was there…and we did it the hard way. We got down in that red North Carolina dirt and shoveled it out from under the church by hand.

When God saved me, I promised I'd do anything for Him; and I've never backed down. I can't understand anyone who doesn't want to volunteer and work for the Lord. I don't believe people have to get paid for everything they do for God. When the Lord called me to preach, He didn't mention money. I was called to spread the Gospel.

GOD SEES INDIVIDUALS

Let's go back to the question, *Wilt thou be made whole?* and I want you to notice the word *thou*. Make it personal—*thou* means *you*, not anybody else. Will *you* be made whole? Healing is one-on-one just as salvation is. Nobody can get saved for you; it's a personal thing. Your parents may love you more than anyone else, but they can't get saved for you. You have to be willing to come out of the world of sin and degradation and live for the Lord.

There are thousands of people who attend my crusade services, but God works with each one individually. The Lord will reveal their needs to me one-on-one. He'll tell me things about people that they know I couldn't possibly know, and He'll even give me their initials. Then their faith goes Heaven-high, and they're ready to believe that I'm God's true prophet and that I'm telling them the truth. That's what the gifts of the Spirit are for—extra power to help people. God's gifts of knowledge, wisdom, discerning and all the others are to be used to help people.

Will YOU reach out for a healing today?
Will YOU contend for the faith that was once
delivered to the saints and be made whole?
This is the pouring-out time, and God will
re-create any part of your body and make you
well if you'll only let Him.

MIRACLES ARE REAL

A member of my church was born without
a hipbone, but God created one for her when
I touched her and she fell in the Spirit. When
she got up, God had created a hipbone for her.
Another lady in my church needed an operation on both of her knees; but after prayer, the
Lord gave her two new knees, and man had
nothing to do with it. Will you let the Lord
give you a new hip or a new knee?

I prayed for a preacher who received a fabulous miracle for his heart. Doctors at a famous
medical clinic in America had removed half
of his heart; but when he went back to the
clinic after prayer, the doctors were shocked
at what had happened to him. At least fifteen
doctors and the head of the clinic himself kept
the man there for over five hours as they compared his X-rays taken before his miracle with

those taken after his miracle. Even some of the surgeons who had taken part in the surgery were there, and they were all dumbfounded. After quite some time, the man finally asked the head of the clinic, "Have you ever heard of Ernest Angley?" He nodded that he had. "Well, I went to one of his services, and he prayed for me. That's why I have a whole heart."

The head of the clinic said, "We don't believe in anything like that here."

And the preacher said, "No, Doctor, and God doesn't believe in you guys either."

God only believes in people who believe in Him; so if you don't believe in God, He doesn't believe in you. God is not going to waste His faith or His time on you if you don't believe in Him. The Bible says, **For what if some did not believe? shall their unbelief make the faith of God without effect? God forbid: yea, let God be true, but every man a liar** (Romans 3:3,4).

GOD WILL MAKE YOU NEW

The next two words in the question Jesus asked the crippled man are, *be made.* You have to be made new by God because we were all conceived in iniquities and sins. **Behold, I was shapen in iniquity; and in sin did my mother conceive me** (Psalm 51:5). As we have already studied, Adam and Eve were created in perfection in the image of God, but they lost that image when they sinned; however, once you get saved through the blood of the Lamb, the image of God is yours. You're re-made through a miracle of re-creation.

When Jesus healed people, He made them whole all over. When He saved people, He made them completely new and told them to sin no more. He asked the woman caught in adultery, **Woman, where are those thine accusers? hath no man condemned thee? She said, No man, Lord. And Jesus said unto her, Neither do I condemn thee: go, and sin no more** (John 8:10,11). Jesus represented the whole sinful human race on the Cross; and He told us, **Believe me that I am in the Father, and the Father in me: or else believe me for the very works' sake** (John 14:11).

A BRAND-NEW WOMAN

Mary Magdalene was wonderfully made. She had been a woman of the streets, but the Lord cast seven devils out of her and made her into a beautiful creature. **Now when Jesus was risen early the first day of the week, he appeared first to Mary Magdalene, out of whom he had cast seven devils** (Mark 16:9). Mary loved Jesus with all of her heart, and she was the first one at the sepulchre on Resurrection Day. When she arrived, she thought that the Lord's body had been stolen; and she began to weep. The angels who were there asked her why she was crying, and she answered, **Because they have taken away my Lord, and I know not where they have laid him** (John 20:13).

Mary had no idea that she was about to meet the Master again. **And when she had thus said, she turned herself back, and saw Jesus standing, and knew not that it was Jesus. Jesus saith unto her, Woman, why weepest thou? whom seekest thou? She, supposing him to be the gardener, saith unto him, Sir, if thou have borne him**

hence, tell me where thou hast laid him, and I will take him away. Jesus saith unto her, Mary. She turned herself, and saith unto him, Rabboni; which is to say, Master (John 20:14–16). Mary became a great disciple for Jesus, and she had more faith than most of the apostles. She was at the foot of the Cross when Christ was crucified even though she knew she could be killed at any time, and John was the only apostle who was there with her.

We have to let God make us brand new so we can cry, "Look what the Lord has done!" God allows many things to happen to people to bring them to the place where they're humble enough to receive; but no matter what He does, some people never change. They choose to keep their old, stubborn spirit; and they won't obey God.

THE BLOOD CHANGES PEOPLE

How does God make people new?—through the blood. **And that ye put on the new man, which after God is created in righteousness and true holiness** (Ephesians 4:24). You must will to be made new in righteousness and true holiness through the blood. The Lord is the One who makes you that way; you can't do it yourself.

Until you receive a real born-again experience and it's no longer you living but Christ living in you, the ideas of the Bible will seem so far out of reach to you that you will think you can't possibly measure up to them. But when you become new, you will love God's Word. You'll want to hug it to your bosom, and you'll know that it's the greatest treasure on Earth. On the mission fields, people stand crying on the street corners when we give them a Bible. Many have never had one, and they're thrilled to receive God's Word.

I was raised with the Bible and the woodshed, and both of those things keep the devil down. Psychiatrists and psychologists say that godly discipline will warp children's minds, but that's a lie of the devil; it just regulates their minds. My parents made it clear that they weren't going to have children in their home who did as they pleased. My daddy always said, "As long as you eat my bread and sleep in my bed, you're going to live by my rules." **Train up a child in the way he should go: and when he is old, he will not depart from it** (Proverbs 22:6). When you train children in the Word, they will know the right way whether they serve God or not; and they won't be able to get away from the truth. That's God's real love.

COMPLETE DELIVERANCE IS GOD'S WILL

Let's move to the last word, *whole*—that's the key word in this question, *Wilt thou be made whole?* The devil says, "You know you can't be made whole; everybody has some sort of sickness." Let me remind you again that the Lord healed three or four million Israelites when they came out of Egyptian bondage. When they took Holy Communion as the Lord had instructed them to, He healed them. They killed the lamb and spread the blood on the doorposts, and we must use divine blood to cover the doorposts of our hearts. They ate the lamb's body, but we have the body of Christ. **For we are members of his body, of his flesh, and of his bones** (Ephesians 5:30). Does the Lord want us to be members of His body and not be well?

We have no record of Jesus ever being sick. He dealt with the afflictions of many others when He was here, but He was never sick until He took all of our sicknesses and sins upon Himself. **Who his own self bare our sins in his own body on the tree, that we, being dead to sins, should live unto righteousness: by whose stripes ye were healed** (I Peter 2:24).

COMMIT ALL TO GOD

We have studied and weighed all of the words in this question, *Wilt thou be made whole?* and each one applies to you. Now, you must take time with the scriptures to weigh every word and accept each one. Again, take note of this scripture: **Study to shew thyself approved unto God, a workman that needeth not to be ashamed, rightly dividing the word of truth** (II Timothy 2:15). I'm always pondering the Word. When the Lord moved on me for this teaching, you don't know how many times I went over all of this word for word, letting the Holy Spirit help me and guide me. When you yield to Him, He will give you such understanding.

It's time for us to commit all to God. Paul said, **I know whom I have believed, and am persuaded that he is able to keep that which I have committed unto him against that day** (II Timothy 1:12). Can you say this? Paul committed everything to the Lord even though at one time he admitted he was the chief of sinners. **This is a faithful saying, and worthy of all acceptation, that Christ Jesus came into the world to save sinners; of whom I am chief** (I Timothy 1:15).

Paul got his introduction to Jesus when the Spirit of the Lord knocked him down into the dirt. **And as he** [Paul] **journeyed, he came near Damascus: and suddenly there shined round about him a light from heaven: And he fell to the earth, and heard a voice saying unto him, Saul, Saul, why persecutest thou me? And he said, Who art thou, Lord? And the Lord said, I am Jesus whom thou persecutest** (Acts 9:3–5). Paul was completely changed from that moment on.

Let God change you and make you whole all over. Why do you want to keep struggling with heart trouble, lung trouble, arthritis, cancer, diabetes or AIDS when the Lord wills only good health for you?

YOU HAVE TO BELIEVE TO RECEIVE

If you have any weakness in your body, you can get rid of it today. The Lord is our strength and our salvation. **The LORD is... my God, my strength...the horn of my salvation, and my high tower** (Psalm 18:2). The Lord is our health if we'll let Him be, but you have to let the Lord's will be done— that's the secret of living for and receiving from God.

Some of you have never come to the place where you really believe it's God's will for you to stay well all the time, but God wants you to wake up. The Lord is calling every member of the bridal company to Him in a personal way in this last hour because He is soon coming for His Bride. The Lord doesn't want you to be sick. It doesn't bless Him or anybody else. Only when you're healed can you say, "Praise God, I'm well! The devil couldn't keep me bound! Thank you, Jesus, for your healing blood and for going to the whipping post for me."

What are you doing with all of God's promises? I don't know how many promises are in the Word; but I do know that I use all that I need, and there are still plenty left. With God, I always get wonderful results. Why?— because I believe what He says, and I act it out. I don't give the devil a chance. You can get rid of the devil, but you have to know that you can. Job got rid of the devil long before Jesus came to Earth; and when Jesus was here, He met the devil head-on in the wilderness. He put him to flight for a season, and Jesus was ready for him when he came back again. Read about it in Matthew 4:1–11.

ACCEPT JESUS

The Lord wants to make you whole in your soul, mind and body; but the most important miracle is that for the soul. If you're not yet saved, the Lord has been talking to you; and He's asking, "Will you accept what I paid for on Calvary?" *Thus saith the Lord, I have called you so many times; but you're getting too far from the shore. You're not listening, and you're not hearing; you're giving yourself over to evil and not to righteousness. I call to you this day, but I don't promise to call you another day. I have called and called, and Heaven has worked for you; but you've walked away from it all.*

Jesus wants to know, "Will you leave the world behind today and repent with godly sorrow for all the sins you've committed? If so, I'll wash away all of your sins with my precious blood because it's my Father's will for you to be free."

When you will to get saved, you can be saved; but if you just think that you'll get saved someday, then you won't surrender all. When I went to the altar the night I got saved, I meant business; and God was ready to do business with me. He was calling me to Calvary; and I went to church one person that Sunday night, and I left a new person. I became so different that I had to get used to the new me, and that can happen to you, too.

Say the sinners' prayer right now. *Oh, God, save my soul. I'm so sorry I sinned against you; but I've come home, and I'm going to serve you, Lord, for the rest of my life. I believe the blood of Jesus washes away all of*

*my sins. Come into my heart, Jesus! Come
on in!*

If you meant that prayer, you can say, *Hallelujah! He has come! My sins are all gone!*
The Lord said He would make us pure and
clean. **Though your sins be as scarlet, they
shall be as white as snow; though they be
red like crimson, they shall be as wool**
(Isaiah 1:18).

IT'S YOUR TIME TO BE MADE WHOLE

Now that your sins are gone, you're ready
for healing from Heaven. We all have a
miracle invitation from the Lord, so reach
out and accept that invitation. He's asking,
"Won't you come and be made whole?" The
Lord said if two will agree on any one thing
touching Heaven, **it shall be done for them
of my Father which is in heaven** (Matthew
18:19). If you agree, then I agree with you.

*Lord, you've healed so many who were
dying with AIDS. You've made so many little,
deformed children whole through this Jesus
ministry, and you're ready to make many more
whole. Lord, you're ready to heal people of
cancer, diabetes and other deadly diseases just*

as you've already healed untold thousands.
You've re-created hearts, livers and lungs; and
you've healed lepers. Lord, we give you the
glory for every healing testimony we receive.
Heal! in the name of Jesus. Heal! in the holy
name of the Lord.

Let that healing power go through you. It's
the same power that made me whole that
night so many years ago and has given me
such wonderful health ever since. My miracle
lives inside of me and gives me unbelievable
strength to carry the Gospel to a lost world.
Be thou made completely whole!

Jesus is wonderful, and His ways are past
finding out. **O the depth of the riches both
of the wisdom and knowledge of God!
how unsearchable are his judgments, and
his ways past finding out** (Romans 11:33)!
Through the Word and the Holy Ghost, we
can learn all that we need to know to help us
on this journey.

In the name of Jesus, the Son of the living
God, I cry with all of my heart to you, dear
Child of God, "Be thou made whole!"

THUS SAITH THE LORD

I have given my servant words for you, and my Word is everlasting just like my love and my strength. I am your Creator and your Healer. Only believe and be made whole. Only believe and be strengthened by the might of my hand. If you believe, you can be made whole like I made my servant whole so many years ago. I've lived with him and walked with him, and I've given him health.

Use my faith, not human faith. Use my divinity; it's yours because I paid for you to have it, and it's free. It will bring health to your spirit, health to your body, health for the journey and health to enable you to bring the unsaved into my Kingdom in this your final hour. I'm calling my people and drawing them unto me so they will draw others to me, saith the Lord.

This is your hour of grace and divinity, the hour to receive all that Heaven affords for everything you need. I am here to anoint you and help you because I need you in this hour. I need you to take my love and send it to the ends of the Earth. You're living in the greatest hour that has ever been, the great hour of your Lord. He told you He would come, and He will. Let not your heart be troubled, neither let it be afraid.

About the Author

Reverend Ernest Angley is the pastor and founder of Ernest Angley Ministries with churches in two locations: Ernest Angley's Grace Cathedral in Cuyahoga Falls, Ohio and Grace Cathedral in Akron, Ohio. This Jesus ministry is in the midst of a tremendous worldwide outreach which is spreading the Gospel into many nations by way of crusades, television and the printed page. God has endowed Reverend Angley with special gifts to bring healing for soul, mind and body to people all over the world. He does not claim to be a healer but a witness to the marvelous healing power of Christ. His television programs—"The Ernest Angley Hour" (aired weekly) and "The Ninety and Nine Club" (aired daily)—present the fullness of God's Word and teach the truth about salvation, healing and the baptism in the Holy Ghost.

Check your local listing for times in your area.

Visit our website at www.ernestangley.org

MORE BOOKS
by Ernest Angley

RAPTURED
$3.50

A novel by Ernest Angley about the second coming of Christ based on biblical facts. This timely book could change your life.

FAITH IN GOD HEALS THE SICK
$1.95

An instructive book by Ernest Angley telling not only how to receive physical healing from the Lord, but also how to keep that healing.

UNTYING GOD'S HANDS
$10.00

With amazing frankness the author has dealt with many controversial subjects in this book: the ministry of angels, preparation required for the Rapture, guidelines for dating, sex in marriage, sex outside marriage, masturbation, homosexuality. Many other subjects covering the whole life of man are woven into the underlying theme of how to untie God's hands.

CELL 15
$2.95

The dramatic true story of the imprisonment of Reverend Ernest Angley in Munich, Germany, for preaching the Gospel and praying for the sick.

GOD'S RAINBOW OF PROMISES
$1.95

Precious promises from the Word of God (KJV) to cover your every need now and forever will enhance your personal devotions and prove a great blessing in time of trouble.

THE DECEIT OF LUCIFER
$10.00

Using the Word of God as the only standard, Reverend Angley strips the camouflage of Lucifer's insidious deceit from demonology, seducing spirits and the counterfeit works of God. A culmination of information derived from years of training by the Holy Spirit, this book is a must for anyone who wishes to recognize the deadly pitfalls of the dangerous endtime hour in which we live.

LEECHING OF THE MIND
$10.00

Like parasitic leeches of the jungle that live off the blood of their victims, leeches of the mind sap the life force of reason. Through the gifts of the Holy Spirit, Reverend Angley exposes the inner working of Lucifer in the human mind, revealing the most incredible takeover by Lucifer a person could suffer other than total devil possession of the soul.

THE POWER OF BIBLE FASTING
$10.00

The Power Of Bible Fasting is one of the most thorough books on Bible fasting ever written, an invaluable guide into a deeper walk with God and the reality of His presence.

LOVE IS THE ROAD
$10.00

Through His great and precious promises we receive much from the Lord on His Love Road. The Love Road is a supernatural Road laid out by supernatural power, planned by the Lord God Almighty. Discover how you, too, can walk this marvelous Road into the fullness and greatness of God in this last and final hour.

WEEDS IN EDEN
$10.00

One of God's greatest disappointments: Finding weeds in Eden. *Weeds in Eden* describes the cost to God and man of minds overrun with the weeds of disobedience and rebellion. The price paid by heaven and earth was sorrow, heartache and despair, and the price today is still the same. Let this book help you search out any weeds that would contaminate the Eden of your mind in this last and final hour.

THE UNFORGIVABLE SIN
$10.00

There is a sin not even Calvary can pardon. Once people commit this sin, only doom and damnation await them with no chance ever of heaven. Jesus said, *All manner of sin and blasphemy shall be forgiven unto men, but the blasphemy against the Holy Ghost shall not be forgiven unto men . . . neither in this world, neither in the world to come* (Matthew 12:31, 32)

REALITY OF THE BLOOD: VOL. 1
$10.00

In this enlightened book on divine blood, the unique and insightful author, through the power of the Holy Ghost, opens up amazing revelations about the importance of the blood of Jesus for all people. Those who love God with all their heart will be thrilled to find the marvelous understanding of the blood that has been set down in this book.

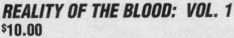

PROSPERITY: SPIRITUAL, PHYSICAL, FINANCIAL...
$10.00
To bring forth the fullness of God's prosperity that we find in His divine will, the writer has gone into the deepness of the Holy Spirit and the Word of God. Prosperity for soul, mind and body is God's will for all His Children.

REALITY OF THE BLOOD: VOL. 2
They used the Blood . . .
We must use the Blood
$10.00
The power in the divine blood of Jesus is being presented in living reality as multitudes experience miracles of healing for soul, mind and body. The Early Church used divine blood through the power of the Holy Ghost, now it's time for the Church in this last and final hour to use the power in the divine blood.

REALITY OF THE BLOOD: VOL. 3
Faith and Feelings!
$10.00
Through the Spirit of God recognize the difference between feelings and faith. Feelings can dishearten you if you rely on them to determine your benefits with God and what you should do for Him. Trusting in feelings is the reason so many Christians have battles of the mind.

REALITY OF THE BLOOD: VOL. 4
Blood Victory Over Disappointments!
$10.00
Realize what is yours through divine blood: freedom
from depression, oppression, sin, sickness, disease
and all other bondages of the devil. Through divine
blood it is possible to overcome Satan's great weapon of
disappointments and take on the mind of Jesus.

THE REALITY OF THE PERSON
OF THE HOLY SPIRIT: VOL. 1
The Holy Spirit in Types and Shadows
$10.00
Reverend Angley lifts the mist curtains of the Old Testament to reveal the Holy Spirit in types and shadows. Let
these marvelous types and shadows come alive in your
heart and thrill your very being.

THE REALITY OF THE PERSON
OF THE HOLY SPIRIT: VOL. 2
The Holy Spirit and Fire
$10.00
The fire of the Holy Spirit includes great miracles of deliverance
as well as the devouring fire of judgment. Read how the fire of
the Holy Spirit will affect your life.

THE REALITY OF THE PERSON
OF THE HOLY SPIRIT: VOL. 3
**The Holy Spirit in the New
and Old Testaments**
$10.00
The Holy Spirit worked throughout the New Testament, but did
He work in Old Testament days? Yes, He did. Read about it in
volume 3 of the Holy Spirit series.

HURRY FRIDAY!
Autobiography of Ernest Angley: Elegant Hardcover Edition
$30.00
Hurry Friday! will make you laugh, cry, and rejoice in the amazing way God has moved in the life of this unique servant of God.

THE MIND OF CHRIST
$10.00
Let this mind be in you, which was also in Christ (Philippians 2:5). What made up His mind? Listed in this book are 141 ingredients found in the mind of Christ.

THE REALITY OF THE PERSON OF THE HOLY SPIRIT: VOL. 4
The Mantle of Power
$10.00
The Bible is filled with examples of the Holy Ghost using the mantle of power through godly men and women. All the truth of God as well as His power is in the mantle. Recognize the blood strength, the greatness, wisdom and knowledge in the glorious mantle of power - and it's for all who will accept it!

LIVING FREE FROM SIN: VOL. 1
$10.00
Is eternal security conditional or unconditional? Can people really live free from sin? This ground-breaking study delves deep into the Scriptures to shed light on a damnable doctrine spreading throughout the world today and reveals what the Bible really has to say about this subject.

BATTLES OF THE MIND
$10.00

Are you tormented with Battles of the Mind? Do you fight depression, oppression, despair and mental misgivings? Are you tormented with the past, present and future or bound with stifling doubt and fear? This book gives you the Bible cure for all that Battles Your Mind!

LIVING FREE FROM SIN: VOL. 2
$10.00

The Bible is filled with the message of Living Free From Sin, and this second volume continues the study of this much-neglected subject. Scripture by scripture, the Lord continues to uncover the damnable doctrine of eternal security in Paul's writings to the Romans, the Corinthians and the Philippians.

REALITY OF THE BLOOD: VOL. 5
Don't Waste The Blood!
$10.00

Jesus Shed His precious blood on Calvary for a lost and dying world, and He intends for us to use it. That blood is man's most powerful weapon, and we must not waste even one, tiny drop. In this profound end-time teaching, Reverend Angley shares an incredible revelation from the Lord on how to use the divine blood to spray the devil into defeat every day. This book will completely change your life!

**IF YOUR BOOKSTORE DOES NOT STOCK THESE BOOKS, ORDER FROM
ERNEST ANGLEY MINISTRIES, BOX 1790, AKRON, OHIO 44309**
You may also order online at www.ernestangley.org

Name _____

Address _____

City _____

State _____ Zip _____

PLEASE SEND ME THE BOOKS INDICATED:

Qty. ____ B1 - Raptured

Qty. ____ B2 - Faith in God Heals the Sick

Qty. ____ B4 - Untying God's Hands

Qty. ____ B5 - Cell 15

Qty. ____ B6 - God's Rainbow of Promises

Qty. ____ B7 - The Deceit of Lucifer

Qty. ____ B8 - Leeching of the Mind

Qty. ____ B9 - The Power of Bible Fasting

Qty. ____ B10 - Love is the Road

Qty. ____ B11 - Weeds In Eden

Qty. ____ B12 - The Unforgivable Sin

Qty. ____ B13 - Reality of the Blood, Vol.1

Qty. ____ B14 - Prosperity: Spiritual,
　　　　　　　　　Physical, Financial...

Qty. ____ B15 - Reality of the Blood, Vol. 2

Qty. ____ B16 - Reality of the Blood, Vol. 3

Qty. ____ B17 - Reality of the Blood, Vol. 4

Qty. ____ B18 - The Reality of the Person
　　　　　　　　　of the Holy Spirit, Vol.1

Qty. ____ B19 - The Reality of the Person
　　　　　　　　　of the Holy Spirit, Vol.2

Qty. ____ B20 - Hurry Friday

Qty. ____ B22 - The Reality of the Person
　　　　　　　　　of the Holy Spirit, Vol.3

Qty. ____ B23 - The Mind of Christ

Qty. ____ B24 - The Reality of the Person
　　　　　　　　　of the Holy Spirit, Vol.4

Qty. ____ B25 - Living Free From Sin, Vol.1

Qty. ____ B26 - Battles of the Mind

Qty. ____ B27 - Living Free From Sin, Vol.2

Qty. ____ B28 - Reality of the Blood, Vol. 5

Qty. ____ B29 - Healing From Heaven, Vol. 1

Amount enclosed $ _____ (Please No C.O.D.s)

DISTRIBUTORS AND BOOKSTORES ORDER FROM:
WINSTON PRESS, BOX 2091, AKRON, OHIO 44309